DARRELL GWYNN: **AT FULL THROTTLE**

DARRELL GWYNN:
AT FULL THROTTLE

TRIUMPHS AND TRAGEDIES FROM A LIFE LIVED AT SPEED

BY ERIK ARNESON

DESIGN BY TOM MORGAN

 **DAVID BULL** PUBLISHING

Dedication

To my wife, Sandy, and my children, Eileen, Kyle, Jaret, and Dakota,
for inspiring me to be a better person every single day of my life.

Acknowledgments

Above all, my heartfelt thanks to the Gwynn family—Darrell, Lisa, Katie, Jerry, and Joan—for allowing me into their lives. Without their willingness to revisit old smiles and cry new tears, this project would never have come to life. Thank you to all those close to Darrell, especially Lisa's parents, Wayne and Adrianne Hurst, Darrell's business manager and friend Bob Abdellah, and Darrell's team of fun-loving attendants. You all made me feel welcome in your lives from the moment I met each of you.

Thank you to David Bull for taking a chance on a first-time author. And a huge thanks to the friends I've made since attending my first NHRA event in 1997 and for the education I received along the way. Thanks to former *USA Today* editor Steve Ballard for giving me the opportunity to cover motor sports and to *USA Today* columnist Jon Saraceno for challenging me and helping me improve as a writer. From the old Winston guard of Denny Darnell, Rob Goodman, and Chad Willis to race team PR reps Jay Wells, Mickey Schultz, Susie Arnold, Dave Ferroni, Joe Sherk, Rob Gieger, Jon and Joanne Knapp, Skip Allum, Woody Woodruff, Rick Vogelin, Jeff Romack, and Judy Stropus. I appreciate my friendship with each of you. A special thanks to Scott Sebastian, who introduced me to Darrell in 1998, and to Dave Densmore, without whose historical assistance and advice I could never have painted a complete picture. Thank you to NHRA director of media relations Anthony Vestal and *National Dragster* managing director Phil Burgess. A special "thanks" to *National Dragster* photo editor Teresa Long for introducing my family to drag racing and for taking the time to search the photo archives with obvious loving care and attention. And thanks as well to Les Welch, Don Gillespie, Auto Imagery, and all the photographers who contributed to the look and feel of this special project.

Also a special thanks to "Tog" at Eurodragster.com and my drag racing friends across the pond, especially Mike Collins and Richard Stirling. Thanks to Darrell's doctors and therapists for their insight, Mike Kerchner at *National Speed Sport News* for opening the magazine's archives, and my friend,Tom Cotter, for creating an environment that encouraged completion of this project in the midst of chaos.

I also would like to acknowledge the NHRA drivers I have interviewed along the way, for this project and countless others. Shirley Muldowney, Kenny Bernstein, John Force, Don Garlits, Dale Armstrong, Frank Hawley, Mike Dunn, and many others never hesitated to take my calls and share their stories. Thanks also to longtime NHRA racer and crew chief Ken Veney and announcer Dave McClelland. It is this drag racing "community" that keeps me coming back for more. There are so many more stories that should be told.

Thanks to my family and friends for all the support and encouragement. Sandy was my number one supporter and first editor, and she and the kids excused my absences from the family to chase my dream of writing this book. And finally—thanks, Mom, for the editing and coaching, and thanks, Dad, for cheering me along the entire way. I love you both.

Library of Congress Control Number: 2003106290

ISBN: 1 893618 33 1

David Bull Publishing, logo, and colophon are trademarks of David Bull
Publishing, Inc.

Book and cover design: Blue Design, Portland, Maine (www.bluedes.com)

Printed in the United States

10 9 8 7 6 5 4 3 2 1

DAVID BULL PUBLISHING
4250 East Camelback Road
Suite K150
Phoenix, AZ 85018

602-852-9500
602-852-9503 (fax)

www.bullpublishing.com

PAGE 2: Wheels up and setting records every run in Dallas before falling in
the final to Don Garlits in 1986. (Darrell Gwynn collection)
PAGE 5: Darrell warms up the car in the pits. (Darrell Gwynn collection)
RIGHT: A Darrell sandwich: the "Kid" between Lisa and Linda Vaughn.
"Enough said," Darrell remarks. (Les Welch)

FRONT COVER PHOTO CREDITS:
Main photo: Darrell Gwynn collection.
Color photos: (left to right) Frank Dinkler, Darrell Gwynn collection; Mark
Mezzano; Darrell Gwynn collection.
BACK COVER PHOTO CREDIT: Les Welch

Fiery crash revs racer's will, spirit

By Maya Bell

SENTINEL MIAMI BUREAU

MIAMI — Darrell Gwynn used to strap himself to a dragster and cover a straight quarter-mile course in less than 5 seconds.

Now he can't push his own wheelchair.

His right arm has limited movement; his left arm is amputated at the elbow. He can't hold his head up without a neck brace. He can't bend his legs without a therapist.

He is, by any physical measure, half the man he was before a fiery crash at a British raceway April 15 crushed his spinal cord. But, by any measure of will or spirit, Gwynn is twice the person, determined to make the most of a life he never contemplated living.

"Most people just lie back and feel sorry for themselves, saying, 'Why me? Why me?'" said neurosurgeon Barth Green, president of the Miami Project to Cure Paralysis. "Not Darrell. He was a winner before the crash, and he's proving he's still a winner."

A drag-racing sensation headed for the 1990 Top Fuel championship, Gwynn, 28, was on top of his world when it crashed and burned Easter Sunday. He was holder of a world record, destined to become a legend, due to marry the 1990 Orange Bowl queen.

Now, with his family, friends and fiancee at his side, Gwynn is bringing more attention to the Miami Project than he ever dreamed. He had chosen the research center as a charitable

Please see **GWYNN, A-12**

PHOTO/TOM SALYER

Darrell Gwynn faces his recovery with a dose of humor: He gets a good laugh as another patient pops a wheelie in a wheelchair.

CONTENTS

Preface by Darrell Gwynn 10

Foreword by Don Garlits 14

Chapter One: One Bad Day in England 16

Chapter Two: From Diapers to Dragsters 24

Chapter Three: Getting Behind the Wheel 36

Chapter Four: The Road to a Championship 50

Chapter Five: Breathin' Nitro 66

Chapter Six: Thirty-five Days of Hell 92

Chapter Seven: Finding a New Normal 108

Chapter Eight: Back on Track 124

Chapter Nine: Miracles and Memories 140

Epilogue 158

Preface

Crashing into a retaining wall at more than 250 mph, there's no time for anything like deep, philosophical thought. You hold on. You hope to survive. Bang, it's done.

Fortunately, I did survive such a hit, but it took a very heavy toll. Plummeting instantly from what was then the highest point of my personal and professional life, I lingered at death's door. A long uphill recovery was immediately before me, an adjustment into a lifestyle I'd never imagined for myself. My world seemed torn apart in every way possible. But given the severity of the accident, I consider myself lucky indeed.

My recovery period offered me plenty of time to consider, "What does it all mean? Why me?" Until then, I'd spent my life living in the moment. I hadn't much cared about trying to understand the "Big Picture," nor even really considered whether there was such a thing. But the months following the accident left time to consider that and more.

Later, people approached me about telling my story in a book. I was flattered, but skeptical that there was anything noteworthy beyond what could already be found in the racing records. So, I rejected those opportunities for a while. Eventually, I began to think differently. Perhaps if I told my story, it would serve as a source of encouragement to others facing major challenges. I'm indebted to Erik Arneson and David Bull for giving me that chance.

So, call it what you like: "luck," "fate," "destiny," or even "God's will." I survived a brush with death and now pursue being a better, wiser, more productive person. My faith in God, active long before the accident, has further solidified and substantially grown in the years since.

My good fortune goes far beyond surviving my injuries at Santa Pod Raceway, and so many of these blessings are things for which I can't remotely take credit. Consider, for example, my parents, Jerry and Joan. I was born into a loving, supportive household, where I was given every opportunity to learn responsibility, build character, and succeed. My parents have been behind me every moment of each day of my life. I can't thank them enough.

Then there's my loving wife, Lisa. Friends since childhood, we grew up under each other's noses. But as adults we had every opportunity for our lives to head in different directions. Boy, am I glad that didn't happen. Lisa is a perfect blend of beauty, smarts, and strength—and she's all mine. With her by my side, I can confidently face any challenge.

Lisa's parents, Wayne and Adrianne, also stepped forward in a big way, making daily sacrifices that allow us to live the most normal life possible under trying circumstances. As I count my blessings, they're forever on my list.

Now, I can absolutely assure you I did have something *very* important to do with the birth of our daughter, Katie! But even Katie's birth must be attributed not just to Lisa and me, and not even just to our families. As you'll learn, Katie's birth was in no small way a medical miracle, enabled by the brilliant and dedicated people of the Miami Project to Cure Paralysis. Never did I dream that my

LEFT: Darrell offers fans his signature salute while backing up after a burnout. (Mark Mezzano, Darrell Gwynn collection) **ABOVE:** Scared to death, a teenage Darrell heads for the staging lanes at Miami-Hollywood Speedway Park for one of his first licensing runs at the wheel of Jerry's AA Altered roadster. (Darrell Gwynn collection)

relationship with the Miami Project, which predated my accident, would come back to benefit me in so many deeply important ways. I believe that through the efforts of the Miami Project, and other institutions like it, people like me will walk again. And as wonderful as that might be, in Katie's birth the Miami Project has already given me a gift beyond words.

Finally, there are the people I consider my friends. There are so very many, it would take a small forest of trees to make the paper necessary to thank them all in writing. Whatever I've done for them through the years has come back to me tenfold.

All of this support has been indispensable to me in both my personal and professional life. One of the primary results is that I'm able to continue my daily role as a professional race team owner. Equally important, Lisa and I recently launched the Darrell Gwynn Foundation—a dream realized. Through it we are assisting research to cure paralysis and otherwise helping those in need.

Do I believe in miracles? Sure do. If you were me, how could you not? As much as we might wish otherwise, we can never completely control the path of our lives. But we surely can strive to make the most of what we're given.

Darrell Gwynn

Foreword by
Don Garlits

I have known the Gwynn family through drag racing for nearly fifty years, so I've known Darrell since he was born. However, I had to read Darrell's biography to truly know the Gwynns' love for one another, devotion to God, and stamina.

Darrell was a young man in the prime of his life and career when he had a horrific crash—to make matters worse, it happened outside of the United States. From this accident Darrell was for all practical purposes paralyzed from the neck down. Since the fifties it has been my belief that there are only two kinds of dragster drivers: those who have crashed and those who are going to crash. Sometimes we walk away from a high-speed accident and sometimes we don't. Darrell is one who didn't.

When it came to Darrell Gwynn versus Don Garlits at the track, I knew that I had to be on my toes because he seemed to be a little extra hungry. I was the one who nicknamed him "the Wolf" because of how aggressive he was when we matched up against each other. Darrell was special in the race car, and special to me. Whether he beat me or not, I knew he would do well in the sport. You just had the feeling he was going to be a champion.

Through Darrell's story, readers will better understand the hard work, long hours, costs, and very real dangers that racers face. This book is a must-read for any young individual considering going into professional drag racing. I would also like to hope that Darrell's experience will make inspirational reading for anybody with disabilities, especially those who use a wheelchair.

I came away from reading the book marveling at the determination of Darrell's family, his fiancée, his friends and fellow racers, and, most of all, Darrell himself. His faith in God and strong relationships with family and friends gave him the strength to move forward. This inspiring biography explains how he coped with his tragic accident, returned his team to racing, and learned to cope with life from a wheelchair.

Of course, the Darrell Gwynn story is not finished, and every day brings Darrell and his family new challenges and unanticipated joys. We should all hold Darrell and his family up in our prayers to give them strength of body and mind: Jerry, Joan, Lisa, Darrell, and, of course, their miracle baby, Katie. These people are remarkable human beings and I am proud to call them my friends.

LEFT: "Big Daddy" Don Garlits and Darrell share a moment before the 1985 final at Indy. "It doesn't get any better than this," Darrell says of racing against one of his childhood heroes. (Darrell Gwynn collection)
ABOVE RIGHT: "Big Daddy" Don Garlits suffered a dramatic blowover against Darrell at Englishtown in 1986 at the peak of their rivalry. (Darrell Gwynn collection)

Chapter One: One Bad Day in England

Eddie's Deli is one of those great places in America you get to experience only if someone happens to take you there.

Tucked away on a crooked South Florida backstreet, dwarfed in the shadow of Lee's Automotive in the 33-square-mile town of Davie, Eddie's looks like it could seat about thirty if everyone inhaled, but most customers seem content grabbing a sandwich and heading back to work. Firemen, mechanics, construction workers—you don't see a lot of suits and ties walking in and out.

A mural painted on the building's cinder block front depicts a man on horseback before a mountain range that probably ranks as the tallest in the Sunshine State. It's noticeably out of place in an area where the highest peaks are concrete causeways spanning the numerous man-made canals and waterways.

Inside, the people are friendly, the chicken salad is fresh, and the entire place is so clean, you'd think the first sandwich has yet to be made. The interior is decorated with trace amounts of Western paraphernalia. One of Florida's few remaining "cowboy towns," Davie's frontier history and rodeo roots are pinned between the eclectic craziness of Miami's South Beach and the aging wealth of Palm Beach.

The cowboy motif is disturbed by one small item—an autographed 8 by 10 photo of drag racer Darrell Gwynn that hangs on the wall, a handout "hero card" from the late 1980s when "the Kid" was taking the high-powered National Hot Rod Association

(NHRA) by storm. Darrell, a Miami native whose race shop is located in Davie, is the resident celebrity at Eddie's, and when he rolls in for lunch, everyone knows the routine.

One of Darrell's attendants clears a space at the front table for the wheelchair and disappears into a storage room to retrieve something shaped like a license plate. It has the words "Do not throw away" scribbled on one side and "property of DG" on the other. The plate is then taped to the front of the air-conditioning vent.

Paralyzed from the chest down, Darrell struggles to regulate his body temperature. A cool breeze, welcomed by most in the tropical South Florida humidity, is painfully uncomfortable for him.

Darrell orders vegetable soup, a turkey sandwich, and a large bag of his junk-food Achilles' heel—potato chips. A series of straps and a strategically bent spoon are attached to his right hand and he goes to work on the soup and chips, getting a little help with the sandwich from his attendant.

Everyone who walks into the place seems to know Darrell, stopping for a few minutes to ask about the race team or just to say hello. Strangers, on the other hand, never make the connection between the small, autographed 8 by 10 hanging on the wall and the man in the wheelchair munching on chips. That connection was broken years earlier and more than 4,000 miles away. One bad day in England had changed everything.

The trip in the spring of 1990 was to be nothing more than a business venture for Darrell and his father, Jerry. It would be the third year the father-son combo would gather a couple of car buddies and make the transatlantic flight. The plan was to meet New Jersey

[17]

LEFT: All alone on the track for an exhibition pass, Darrell prepares for launch at Santa Pod on April 15, 1990. (Mike Collins) **ABOVE:** Moments before climbing into his car on Easter Sunday 1990, Darrell spends a few moments with his father, Jerry. (Mike Collins)

drag racer and race promoter Harlan Thompson at England's famed Santa Pod Raceway for the Easter Thunderball, a traditional holiday feast of European hot-rodding.

The deal was simple. The Gwynns sold Thompson their Top Fuel dragster from the previous NHRA season, hawked a handful of hats and T-shirts, and applied the money made toward new equipment for the current racing season. Between the car, a small appearance fee, and souvenir sales, the annual trip netted the Gwynns somewhere in the neighborhood of $75,000.

"The bottom line was that it was good for the team," Darrell says. "I could start out the year with all-new parts and have an outlet for getting rid of my old ones. It was just another business transaction for me. I never thought about the possible consequences of racing over there. It was all business. We flew over, checked into the hotel, and headed straight for the track."

The 1990 visit to Santa Pod was sandwiched between NHRA events at home. After racing in the season opener in Pomona, California, collecting his second Gatornationals Top Fuel title at his home track in Gainesville, Florida, and scoring a runner-up finish at the Winston Invitational all-star event, there were a few open weeks before the team was to race again in Atlanta. So Darrell and Jerry grabbed close friends Carl Ruth and Chris Hyatt and jumped on a plane.

"We'd bring a couple of guys along to crew, just in case the car needed any work once we got over there," Darrell says. "But mostly it was just to have fun with some friends and give them a chance to see another part of the world."

Jerry, who spent nearly three decades with Standard Oil and then Chevron as a fleet mechanic and construction manager, had retired two months earlier with plans to go racing with his son full-time. The elder Gwynn, an NHRA Super Eliminator world champ in 1969, had spent countless long weekends crisscrossing the Southeast in the sixties and seventies with Darrell at his side, never reaching the level of success in drag racing's elite classes needed to make a living at the track. Now, with Darrell behind the wheel of the family race car, the goal of having the baddest hot rod on the planet certainly appeared within reach.

It was the 15th of April—Easter Sunday—when Darrell, Jerry, and the guys began preparing the Coors Extra Gold hot rod for the short exhibition run at the Pod. Darrell was alone on the track in the left lane, with plans to make a little noise, get down the track, and shut it off.

The conditions that day were right off a British postcard. Overcast, with a threat of light rain, the wind was blowing and a slight chill was in the air. The track itself, located about 30 miles from London in rural Bedfordshire, was constructed in 1966 on the grounds of an old American air base. Europe's first permanent drag racing facility, storied Santa Pod continues to play host to the FIA European Drag Racing Championships and several "run what you brung" events, including the Easter Thunderball.

"The place reminded me of a lot of the tracks we ran in the 1960s," Jerry says. "It was at the end of a long winding country road. The pit areas were only partially paved, with ruts and potholes all over the place. The bleachers were made of wood. It just looked old, but the track itself was decent."

There were plenty of reasons for Darrell to wave off the run that day. It was only an exhibition, and the weather was certainly becoming a factor as a light mist began to coat the surface of the track. Darrell also was lacking some of the safety equipment he normally insisted on, having lent his gloves and arm restraints to Al Segrini, a fellow

ABOVE: Just weeks before traveling to Santa Pod, Darrell was in Charlotte, North Carolina, looking at property with friends Johnny Hayes and Jay Wells. (Darrell Gwynn collection) **RIGHT:** Darrell talks with fellow racer Al Segrini at Santa Pod Raceway outside of London. (Darrell Gwynn collection)

drag racer who had just made an exhibition pass in front of Darrell in one of the Gwynns' old Budweiser-sponsored cars.

"But we had a commitment," Darrell remembers. "There were a lot of fans in the stands and we didn't want to disappoint anyone. We never planned to make a full pass, so it never should have been a big deal. I felt like we at least owed the crowd an attempt to get down through there."

No stranger to the Pod, Darrell had been part of the track's first side-by-side five-second run a year earlier, edging Liv Berstad with a 1/4-mile elapsed time of 5.78 seconds to Liv's 5.84. So, comfortable with the facility, Darrell went through his normal prerace routine, dressing in his fire suit and boots, walking around the car, checking the parachutes, looking for loose spark plug wires or anything else that might appear out of place. Once in the car, Darrell donned his neck collar and Jerry tightened the restraint system so tight that Darrell and the car became one and the same. The only thing missing was that restraining system of straps, connected to D rings on

Darrell's shirtsleeves, that attached to the seat belt system. The straps allowed just enough movement for Darrell to steer the car and activate the parachutes needed to stop the 4,000-horsepower machine at the end of the 1/4-mile strip.

Then there was the handshake.

It was a tradition between father and son that had started years earlier at Miami-Hollywood Speedway Park when Darrell was sitting behind the wheel of Jerry's AA Altered roadster for the first time. On an Altered car, the engine could be placed slightly rearward for better weight distribution. The fastest cars in the Altered category were the AAs with their supercharged engines and fearsome power-to-weight ratios. Strapped in and tucked behind the monstrous cowl, Jerry sensed Darrell's nervousness and offered his hand as comfort as he gave his son last-minute instructions. The gesture became a signature prerace ritual and continued throughout Darrell's driving career.

So Jerry and Darrell shook hands as always, as Darrell prepared to make the run at Santa Pod. Strapped in and ready to go, Darrell and Jerry were being hurried along by race control, but Jerry wanted to wait for Segrini to bring back Darrell's equipment.

Darrell didn't wait, telling Jerry: "Don't worry about it, Dad. We won't be going that fast and I'm just going to shut it off at three-quarters track."

Darrell staged the car and watched the lights drop on the starting pole, known as the Christmas tree, as he had done hundreds of times before.

Yellow. Yellow. Yellow. Green.

As Darrell accelerated off the line in his Coors Extra Gold rocket, the car shook the tires—just a little.

"About a million things were going through my mind," Darrell says. "But I felt like, 'These people are here to see a show, so I need to get back on it and try to make a decent run out of it.' So, I got back

in the gas, drove it for a few hundred more feet, and right about the time I felt I was going to shut it off, the car broke in half and veered toward the wall."

Months earlier, the team had raised the motor angle a few inches in an effort to deliver more weight to the rear wheels. With that, the oil pump had been forced against the framework engine well, so the team adjusted the chromium molybdenum steel framing around the 500-cubic-inch supercharged engine, welding the rails into new positions to accommodate the adjustment.

As Darrell's car lifted on the left side and angled toward the guardrail 982 feet into the run, it was terribly clear that something in the area of the work done months earlier had failed. The problem might have been caused by the adjustments made to the Mike Kase chassis (a common practice among teams seeking every possible advantage), or perhaps it was the result of stress fractures sustained during the dragster's transatlantic voyage.

The car's front end crumpled upon impact with the rail, breaking the car in half and spinning the front end of the dragster counterclockwise, the back end of the driver's compartment slamming into the rail again. The 240-mph whiplash snapped Darrell's neck at the C5 and C6 vertebrae, causing a burst fracture of the fifth vertebra, splintering bone, and bruising the spinal cord. Instantly paralyzed, Darrell's hands came off the steering wheel and without the restraints he normally would have been wearing, his arms waved out of control and out of the cockpit.

As the car erupted in a ball of fire and skidded on its side to a stop, Darrell's left arm was dragged along the asphalt surface of the track and pinned under the frame rail wreckage. His face, left vulnerable when the whiplash flipped his visor out of position, was stinging with first-degree burns.

Jerry watched the nightmare unfold from the starting line. But he had seen numerous accidents over his twenty-five-year racing career, and this one didn't appear as horrific as it was to become.

The Santa Pod fire and rescue crew was first to the car. "A small fuel fire had to be extinguished where the fuel tank had split," recalls Nigel Anniwell, a member of the fire and rescue team Darrell

[21]

LEFT: Darrell makes his way to the car for his exhibition run at Santa Pod. It was the third transatlantic trip Darrell and Jerry had made to sell equipment overseas. (Dick Parnahm) ABOVE: The run at Santa Pod started badly as Darrell smoked the tires before getting back into it as he tried to salvage a decent pass. (Dick Parnham)

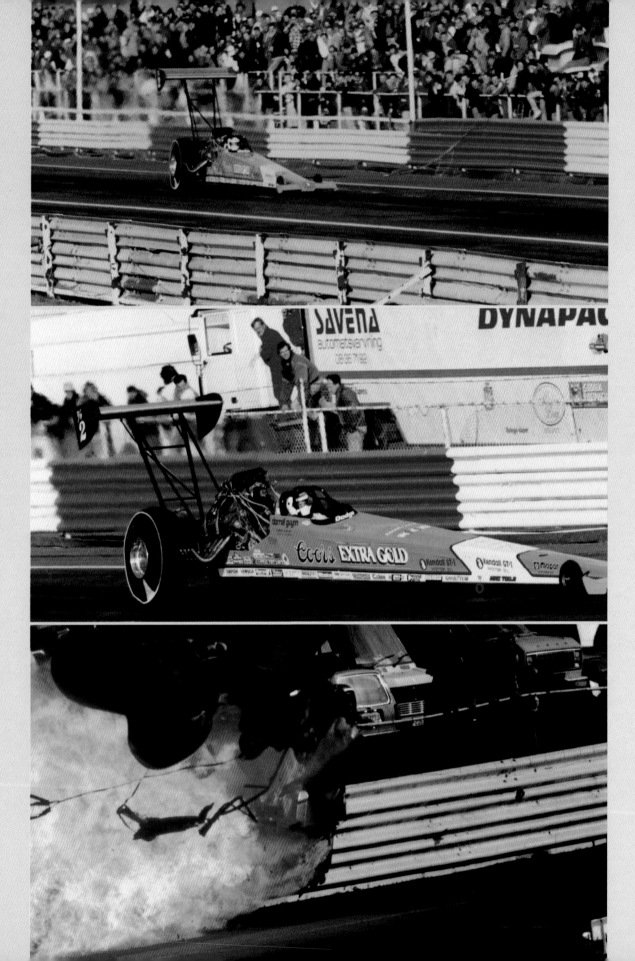

credits with saving his life. "The first concern upon arriving at the crash scene was getting the fire under control and finding out how badly Darrell was injured.

"The accident scene was quite scary," Anniwell adds. "The engine had come out of the car and was sitting on the other side of the track. But everyone at the scene knew exactly what to do. When we reached Darrell, we did not know we were dealing with spinal injuries, but as a matter of precaution, he was treated by the medical team as if he had spinal injuries."

Jerry, Carl Ruth, and Chris Hyatt had followed close behind in a van the team was using to retrieve the car after each run. Carl, after racing through an obstacle course of car parts left littering the track, jumped out of the van and yelled to Darrell. "I shouted to him and asked if he could hear me," Ruth remembers. "He responded and said he was having trouble seeing. The visor was black from the fire and still partially blocking his vision. When I lifted his visor, I asked him if he was OK. He said he thought so, but he couldn't feel his legs."

When Jerry made it to the car, he wanted things to move faster. "When I got down there, he was bleeding profusely from his arm, and they were trying to get an inflatable tourniquet on him," Jerry remembers. "It was then that I realized that the track wasn't prepared for this kind of accident. He was trapped in the car and there was nothing to cut him out with. There was no backboard to put him on. There was no neck collar."

Conscious through the entire ordeal, Darrell felt only the pain on his face. Disoriented and confused, he had yet to realize the magnitude of his injuries.

"When the car finally stopped and my arm was bleeding and trapped under the car, I didn't know why I couldn't move my legs or why I couldn't move my arms," says Darrell, whose helmet and roll cage never suffered a single scratch. "I couldn't figure out why I couldn't get my seat belts off. It had always been so easy to release them thousands of times before and I just couldn't get my hand to work the belts. I couldn't feel my legs, but it never occurred to me that I might be paralyzed. I assumed I was just in shock."

Then Darrell, still feeling only the pain from the burns, looked over and saw his 6-foot, 3-inch, 250-pound father leaning against the guardrail, slumped over, head in hands.

Says Darrell: "That's when I knew things were bad."

ABOVE LEFT: Fans watch in horror as Darrell's Top Fuel dragster explodes into a fireball after breaking apart and slamming into the retaining wall. (Dick Parnham) ABOVE RIGHT: Despite major breakage to many parts of the car, Darrell's driver compartment was still intact after the accident. (Roger Gorringe, courtesy Darrell Gwynn collection)

Chapter 2: From Diapers to Dragsters

Darrell remembers little of his father's earliest drag racing days, which started when Darrell was just a few months old. But he became a regular at South Florida tracks like Masters Field and then Miami-Hollywood Speedway Park while he was still in diapers. Falling asleep in his parents' arms as they drove home from the track late at night and eating at local diners with a table full of friends serve as Darrell's only memories from the days when Jerry was piloting his 1949 British Ford Anglia down South Florida's 1/4-mile tracks.

In 1968, when Darrell was just six, Jerry started toying with the idea of building his first-grader a "junior dragster." A scaled-down front-engine machine, it was a project that took nearly a year to complete, as Jerry tinkered with it in his spare time. With no plans or drawings to work from, he built the entire car from scratch. "I thought it would be cool if Darrell had his own little dragster," Jerry recalls. "I made the frame by brazing 1/2-inch electrical metallic tubing [EMT] together. It had a live-axle rear end, a slipper clutch that was activated when he pushed the pedal down. Even if he messed up, the car would stop if he took his foot off the pedal. We put in a hand brake, and the front wheels had 20-inch bicycle tires." Complete with a 2.5-horsepower Briggs & Stratton engine, Jerry hand-finished the aluminum body and painted it at his Standard Oil shop. For looks, he added a double set of headers to both sides of the retired lawnmower power plant, "making it look bigger than it really was." A family friend added the finishing touch to the red machine. With a smil-

ing devil's face and the words "Red Devil," the first junior dragster was ready to race.

Jerry blocked off the street in front of the house, while Darrell and neighborhood buddy Mark Robinstraw took turns behind the wheel. But it was taking the pint-size hot rod to Miami-Hollywood Speedway Park and making a few runs down a real drag strip that made it special.

The first 1/4-mile pass took 43.11 seconds at a top speed of 23 mph. The second pass was a little better, finishing in 42.43 seconds at 25.02 mph.

"Here we are going down the track at 25 or 30 mph," Darrell says. "Talk about something cool that no other kid in the world got to experience at that time—no other kid had a car like that." The seed was planted.

"I remember living on a corner lot with cars slowly driving by at all hours to see what was going on," Darrell says. "Our house had all the action—lots of cars in the driveway. Every once in a while, people might get to see a race car fired up in the front yard. Everyone knew where the Gwynns lived."

In August 1970, a few days before his ninth birthday, Darrell got a big box from his parents. Tearing into the wrapping, the towheaded kid with the easy smile was a little perplexed to find a suitcase. It didn't take long, however, for the gift's special message to sink in. Jerry and Joan were taking Darrell and his new suitcase to Indianapolis for the U.S. Nationals, the Super Bowl of drag racing. He has missed only one since.

"Before my first trip to Indy, I was the kid thumbing through

LEFT: Darrell gets a ride with Randy Tissot on Kiddie Ride Night at Hialeah (Florida) Speedway. (Darrell Gwynn collection) **ABOVE:** Long before Junior Dragsters were mass-produced and readily available, Darrell got the chance to test drive the homemade "Red Devil" on 116th Street and Northwest 10th Avenue in their Miami neighborhood. The car was designed and built by Darrell's father, Jerry. (Darrell Gwynn collection).

[25]

magazines like *Hot Rod*, *Drag Racing USA*, and *National Dragster*," Darrell says. "I was into all the California racing, and it seemed so cool. When you picked up these magazines and read about 'Wild Willie' Borsch, Don 'the Snake' Prudhomme, and Tom 'the Mongoose' McEwen out in California, you just felt like there was another world out there." As he got older, Darrell's love for all that was drag racing grew with each visit to the 1/4 mile.

After the 1970 U.S. Nationals, young Darrell became a part of drag racing just as much as it was becoming a part of him. The heroes from the pages of his magazines came to life that year at Indy.

Prudhomme, a poster boy for California cool, would win his second consecutive Indy Top Fuel title in 1970, defeating Jim Nicoll in a wild final. A clutch explosion put Nicoll over the guardrail at more than 200 mph, while his engine and the other half of his slingshot dragster slid nearly the length of a football field.

"I wasn't paying much attention to the mechanical side of things back then," Darrell says. "I didn't have much interest in getting my hands dirty. I just liked the glory side. I was running around collecting hero cards and autographs. I was a big dreamer—the kid looking through the hole in the fence, being only 30 feet away from guys like

LEFT: Jerry and Darrell clean up nice for a wedding in 1964. BELOW: Darrell poses next to one of Jerry's first hot rods in 1964. BOTTOM LEFT: Darrell sits at the wheel as Jerry waits to run at nearby Masters Field in Miami. (Darrell Gwynn collection).

Don Garlits, and thinking how cool it must be to be doing what he was doing. I wanted to be right there."

Life around the Gwynn house in the 1960s and early 1970s was quite predictable. Just after dinner, while the dishes were still drying, regulars like Bob Bridges and Ronnie Hughes would be joined by other family friends after working their full-time day jobs, chat for a few minutes, and head to the one-car garage. Some were there to work on the race car. Some were there to hang out with friends. It didn't matter, they all were welcome.

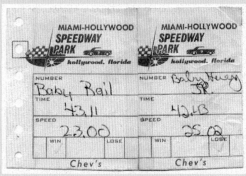

CLOCKWISE, FROM TOP LEFT:
Jerry and Joan pose with Darrell—the swing wasn't too far from the garage in the background. • Time slips for the "Red Devil" junior dragster show the elapsed time for each run. • Darrell breaks out his earliest street rod—a gold Schwinn Stingray equipped with noisemaking baseball cards attached to the rear spokes. (Darrell Gwynn collection) • Three views of Darrell and Jerry testing the "Red Devil" at Miami-Hollywood Speedway Park to see what their little hot rod could do at the track.

[27]

On local race weekends, racers like Garlits, Herb Parks, and members of Raymond Beadle's crew were regular houseguests, sleeping in the bedroom next to Darrell's. "Jungle Jim" Lieberman stopped by, sharing clutch secrets with Jerry. No-names or big names, they all seemed to visit Darrell's father at one time or another.

"There's a lot of different kinds of people that drive race cars," Darrell explains. "My father was the kind of racer that knew every part of his cars, built his own cars, worked on his own cars, and drove his own truck. My dad built everything—from the trailer that hauled the cars to the house that we lived in.

"It was a lot simpler then," he adds. "It wasn't like, 'Hey, let's go put this motor on the dyno and see if it will make enough power for us to qualify.' It was, 'Let's take this old motor out of this car that we got from the junkyard, put a different manifold and carburetor on it, and go run it.'"

Still too young to be concerned with the mechanical details of what was going on in the garage, Darrell was content to enjoy the cars and mimic the sounds of speed he heard by putting baseball cards in the spokes of his yellow Schwinn. But he knew there was something special about all the activity going on nearly every night around the house.

In 1971, the Gwynns moved to Biscayne Gardens in North Miami, three houses removed from Interstate 95, into what the family refers to as "a six-car garage with a diner attached."

Joan went without some of the niceties of home decorating, leaving the living room bare of furniture for a time because any extra money was put into the race team. On Saturdays, when the team wasn't racing, it was Joan who made fifteen grilled-cheese sandwiches to feed a crew of guys doing everything from working on the race car to building trailers or tire racks.

Although Jerry's time in the powerful and unpredictable AA Altered and alcohol Funny Cars made Joan nervous at times, she never worried about Darrell. She knew Jerry would make sure everything

MIAMI SPEEDWAY PARK, Hollywood, Fla. — Former NHRA World Champion Jerry Gwynn showed his stuff at the Miami strip, and handily won Competition Eliminator with a fine 8.34, 149.00 mph scorching of R. J. Smith's A/Altered at 8.88, 154.37.

was as safe as it could be, and she wanted nothing more than to see her son believe in himself and chase his dreams.

"My childhood was very painful. I was raised to be seen and not heard," Joan says. "I was always told all my ideas were stupid, and I vowed never to do that to Darrell. I vowed that my children would have confidence and praise. I encouraged Darrell to follow his dreams, do the best he could at everything he did, and if nothing else, he was going to feel loved."

Looking back, Darrell realizes just how much everyone gave up to go racing.

"Though we never went hungry, Mom and Dad both sacrificed a lot so my dad could do what he loved," Darrell says. "I don't think my mom had her first new car until 1990, when my dad retired. Dad

had a friend who owned a junkyard, and he would find cars there that had been stolen or repossessed and fix them up.

"One of Mom's nicest cars was a 396 Chevelle that didn't have seats, wheels, or a radio when they bought it. Dad picked it up for next to nothing and put bucket seats in it, and here's my mom tooling around in a 396 Chevelle in big hair and big sunglasses.

"My parents didn't just go out and buy stuff. Dad would work for it, earn it, or work a job off for it. There was a lot of robbing Peter to pay Paul and horse-trading going on in those days."

By 1973, when he was twelve, Darrell's interest in racing continued to grow. So did his interest in making money, as he managed to do enough yard work around his North Miami neighborhood to stockpile a bank account approaching a few thousand dollars. Taking money-management tips from his parents, Darrell dipped into his stash only for "important" things like tools, go-karts, and minibike motors.

An off-weekend trip to a nearby aircraft junkyard, Simmons Surplus, led to his first venture on the business side of racing. "They

had old wrecked airplanes there, but more important, they had barns and barns full of the trickest fasteners and fittings you ever saw in your life," Darrell remembers. "Here we were picking up things at a junkyard that looked California trick when we showed up at the track."

Then Darrell spotted his pot of gold. Up until the mid-1980s, racers didn't take clutches out between rounds, they simply cooled them with tiny 12-volt fan motors from old junked cars.

"We ran across these 'clutch coolers' with aluminum housings that were used for something else on the airplanes," Darrell explains. "There was a stack of just hundreds of them—dirty and nasty and covered with cobwebs. We cleaned one up and tried it as a clutch cooler. We plugged that thing in, and it just hummed and blew so much air. It was the coolest clutch cooler ever. So, we used it for the weekend, and I came up with the idea of selling them to other drivers."

Darrell, who had paid $10 for the first cooler, went back to Simmons Surplus and talked them into selling him a wagon load at $5 apiece.

"Here I am at eleven or twelve years old, wheeling around my clutch coolers at the U.S. Nationals or Gatornationals in my little wagon, selling them to all the Mac Daddies of drag racing for $20 each," Darrell says. "I was known as 'the clutch cooler kid' and I'd make more money at the U.S. Nationals than my dad did if he went out first round. I think I made $800 at Indy one year.

"When you're a kid walking up to a superstar and money is changing hands and they know your first name or they know your dad's name, it is an incredible feeling," he adds. "The phone rings at home at night, and it's some hotshot racer on the other end looking for Darrell and wanting to buy one of my clutch coolers. How cool is that?"

Darrell took his marketing savvy to the next level throughout his mid-teens, painting the clutch coolers to match the color schemes of specific cars. Blue for Beadle's "Blue Max." Orange for Gary Burgin's

TOP LEFT: Newspaper clipping—family night out for the Gwynns.
LEFT: Darrell helps Jerry and family friend Bob Bridges (left) work on cylinder heads for Jerry's car in July 1975. (Darrell Gwynn collection)
RIGHT: Washing Jerry's race car was one of the after-school chores Darrell and his friends often performed around the garage. (Darrell Gwynn collection)

Darrell that he ought to be getting contingency money—payouts provided by corporate sponsors to racers displaying their decals—when he won races.

Traveling with his dad and a few family friends on Smoker Smith's East Coast Fuel Funny Car circuit, a series of drag events put on by promoter Tom "Smoker" Smith, wasn't all fun and games. A typical weekend trip might begin Friday night and cover three no-name tracks in several states, plus stops for an occasional mall appearance. On a good weekend, if nothing broke, the team went home with about $1,800—a nice chunk of change in the seventies. Often the team would pull into the Gwynn driveway at 4 A.M. on Monday morning, just in time for Darrell to shower and head back to school. Despite the grueling schedule, Darrell had to score Cs or better in all his classes. The same rules applied for any of Darrell's friends who wanted to tag along.

"But not everybody thought it was great having a kid hanging around," Darrell recalls. "One guy who helped Dad, Bob Bridges, didn't have a lot of patience for a twelve-year-old punk bouncing around in the car wanting to stop at South of the Border while they're trying to get to a racetrack, or terrorizing the motel room, jumping on the beds 'till they broke."

One year at the U.S. Nationals, Bridges got so tired of Darrell's constant chattering that he wrapped Darrell's arms and legs in duct tape, propped him up against the tailgate of Jerry's truck, and walked away.

"Orange Baron." Black for Big Daddy and for Segrini, one of Darrell's best salesmen.

"I don't think I ever painted one pink," Darrell says. "But I must have sold one to Shirley Muldowney at some point."

A friend of Jerry's was in the printing business and made stick-

ers for Darrell to put on his products:

Driver Dale Armstrong, one of Darrell's favorites, was one of several competitors to carry the decal on his car and often joked with

"He just left me there," Darrell remembers with a chuckle. "People were walking by, pointing at me, laughing and taking pictures. He left me there for what seemed like hours."

And a lot of the tracks the Gwynns visited were not exactly the safest play areas for kids, especially when the sun started to go down—tracks like Blaney Drag Strip in Elgin, South Carolina, or Warner Robbins Dragway in Georgia, or others in towns most people have never heard of.

"We went to one track in Alabama that was unbelievable," Darrell recalls. "On one side of the racetrack it went straight up, and on the other side it went straight down and there were no guardrails. People parked along the strip all the way down, sitting on their tailgates. The track was on the way to another race and the promoter paid us $300 to do a half-ass run at three-quarters speed, so we did it.

"Nine times out of ten, if the place had a tower, a Christmas tree, and two lanes, we were good to go," Darrell says. "At some of those tracks, it was just as common for the ambulance to tend to someone getting stabbed or punched somewhere in the bleachers as it was to help a racer that had been in a wreck. Other places had fans throwing beer bottles onto the racetrack. I would feel my chest tighten every time Dad got ready to race.

"Some of these places didn't even have lights at the end of the track, so once the cars got past the finish line, we couldn't see them," Darrell says. "Mom would have to drive down with her high beams on to pick up Dad. There was one time we were driving down to look for Dad and the guy he was racing was off in a ditch upside down. We found Dad and brought him back while they were cutting the other guy out of his car."

Though sometimes a little frightening, all of the small town racing experiences had a profound effect on Darrell's childhood.

"I'd like to get a directory and think about all the little Podunk racetracks that I've been to," says Darrell, who watched his dad pilot the family Funny Car to twenty-nine wins in thirty-seven events

on the match-race circuit. "I have just as many memories from those places as I do from Indy or the Gatornationals. There's a story behind each one of them."

At home, Darrell's after-school chores were a little different from those of his classmates. Sure, he mowed the lawn and picked up after himself, but he also washed engine blocks and scrubbed pistons and rods and fitted rings, if necessary—anything to get the race car ready for Jerry, Bob, Ronnie, and the boys before they came home from work.

In his early teen years, the garage chores meant nothing more than extra work, but as time went on, Darrell wanted to be a bigger part of the process.

"I grew up around it—I lived with it," Darrell says. "I had to go out and wash parts every night, so when I got to the races, it really didn't interest me until I was about fourteen or fifteen. That's when

I started to get my hands dirty, working on the engine, taking the cylinder heads off, taking the headers and the wheels off, and just being an active part of the routine at the races. At times, there was a lot of work to be done."

It was then that Darrell began carving his niche on the family race team. "Dad would say 'OK, son, when you get home from school, unload the car, jack it up, and put it on jack stands,' and there would be a list of things for me to do," Darrell says.

Back at the track, Jerry started letting Darrell warm the car up; sitting in the seat, he began to get familiar with his surroundings. Darrell did his work in the team's pit area, but would often wander off at some point to catch a ride in Garlits's tow vehicle or hang out in Armstrong's pit area.

"One of the people I really enjoyed being around as a youngster was Armstrong," Darrell says. "As a teenager, I spent as much time at Dale's car as I did at my dad's car. At the end of the day, when everything was loaded up, Dad and Mom would drive over to Armstrong's

pit and find me. Bob Bridges would be grumbling because I should have helped load up, but they always knew where to find me."

It was Armstrong who would buy Darrell his first Simpson fire suit, helmet, and gloves.

"He was just so young and enthusiastic," Armstrong remembers. "When I was a kid growing up in Canada, we played a lot of hockey and they called us 'rink rats.' Darrell was a pit rat, just totally absorbed by anything to do with drag racing. I guess I took to him because he reminded me so much of myself at his age—full of youthful energy and enthusiasm."

"I think it was just Darrell's personality and his desire to check everything out that kept the guys from running him off," Jerry says. "We never knew exactly where he was at the end of the day, but we knew there were only a few places to choose from."

Darrell's childhood was not limited to drag racing activities. He played Little League baseball, went fishing in the canals near his home, and raced around empty neighborhood lots on his Kawasaki

DeSoto ⚜ Memorial SPEE

100, occasionally catching motocross legend Roger DeCoster racing at Amelia Earhart Field in nearby Hialeah. But his mind was always on getting back to the 1/4 mile.

"I was just out there thinking about racing," Darrell says. "Not that I was thinking about driving, but things like what race we were going to next, what city we were going to. Whether it was Little League or school or anything else, it just felt like it was interrupting what I really wanted to be doing."

During high school, Darrell worked part-time at the Stripper, a metal-stripping company in Opa Locka owned by a friend of Jerry's. Soon after Darrell graduated from North Miami Senior High, another family friend, Bill Wynne, helped him land a job at PIECO (Petroleum Industrial Equipment Company), rebuilding gas pumps and

doing anything else they could find for him.

"Being friends of my dad, these guys let me go racing on the weekends," Darrell says. "They understood these weren't jobs I wanted to do full-time, so they let the job fit in with the racing. Half the time, these guys would go to the races with us."

Darrell made a half hearted attempt at college, attending Miami-Dade Community College, which was built, ironically, on land that was once Masters Field, the drag strip Darrell first visited as a toddler. After two months Darrell withdrew, deciding school wasn't for him, and told his father, "I'm just wasting my time and your money."

"I tried to tell him that it wasn't a very smart decision," Jerry says. "But he said he was going to be the best drag racer out there ... and for a while, he was."

ABOVE: The crew: Darrell and friend Dino Powley join Ronnie Hughes (left), Jerry, Miss Winston, and Bob Bridges after a Division II points meet win. Jerry holds the trophy, while Bob is content to hold the trophy girl. (Darrell Gwynn collection)

Chapter Three:
Getting Behind the Wheel

Five runs into the process of earning his first drag racing license, a few minutes after knocking off a pass at 129 mph in his dad's AA Altered roadster, Darrell wanted to go home and not return to the racetrack for quite a while.

The roadster was dubbed "Baby Huey" after Jerry's friend Dick McFarland called the elder Gwynn a "big, dumb duck." It was a Chrysler-powered challenge to control for even the most experienced driver. It certainly wasn't the safe pick for a skinny seventeen-year-old in search of his first pass to go drag racing.

A short wheel base, alcohol-powered Funny Car chassis with an altered body, and a wing designed to keep the car stable and on the ground, "Baby Huey" was a squirrelly combination at best. The car just wanted to go everywhere.

"The AA Altered was a handful," Darrell says. "Altereds are the most ill-handling cars you can drive down a drag strip, and it's one of those machines I was trying to get my license in."

Jerry's lesson plan, however, was solid.

To safely get Darrell to that final fast pass, he had initially set the throttle to open only a quarter of the way, allowing Darrell to go through his entire routine in the car at a manageable speed. Darrell would hit the gas, work through the gears of the Lenco three-speed transmission, release the parachutes, and shut off the fuel supply. After each run, Jerry would open the throttle a little more, and Darrell would continue through each step of the process.

"I told Darrell that as long as he did exactly what I asked him to do every time, he could keep doing it," Jerry says. "I told him that he had absolutely nothing to prove to me, so if he wanted to quit at any point, we would shut it off. I wanted to make sure it was what he wanted to do. I didn't want him doing any of it for me."

Darrell climbed in and the lessons began. The first run was at 60 mph. The second run: 76 mph. The third run: 101 mph. The fourth run: 129.

"The fifth run just scared the crap out of me," Darrell says. "It wasn't the speed, because I shut off early, but the car was just all out of shape and it really scared me."

The pair packed it in and called it a night, leaving Darrell to make the next move.

Two weeks later, Darrell and Jerry returned to Miami-Hollywood, and Darrell started to feel a little more comfortable in "Baby Huey", chalking up runs between 150 and 181 mph.

"For my licensing run, at around eleven o'clock at night with the dew falling and very few lights, I ran down there at 192 mph in the AA Altered," Darrell says. "That wasn't a bad little run in 1979."

Darrell Mark Gwynn was now a licensed NHRA drag racer.

"Now, I was a kid working for a petroleum company with an NHRA license in my pocket thinking I was hot stuff. All I wanted to know was when I was going to get to drive again," he says.

At the time, however, Jerry was still behind the wheel of the family racing machine. There was no set schedule for Darrell to drive, but

LEFT: Jerry adds Darrell's name to the family race car, giving his son time behind the wheel when opportunities presented themselves. The AA Altered was a handful for even the most experienced driver. (Darrell Gwynn collection) **ABOVE:** Victory lane at the Sportsnationals in Bowling Green, Kentucky, with Jerry, Darrell, Mike Cunningham, and Chris Cunningham. (Darrell Gwynn collection)

[37]

the painted signature by the driver compartment soon switched from "Jerry Gwynn" to "Jerry or Darrell Gwynn," with Jerry driving at national events and Darrell getting seat time at select points meets.

Unsure of his future in the sport, Darrell continued working at PIECO and living at home while tooling around the Southeast with Jerry, waiting for opportunities to drive. In the evenings after dinner, he often escaped for an hour or so by jogging, riding his bike, or fishing until the South Florida sun went down.

It was on one of his evening bike rides that his racing future came into focus. On a summer night in 1980, Darrell happened to take a different route than he usually did, opting to venture out a little farther than his usual two or three times around the block. He found himself riding by the house of Bob Hall, a racer who competed in the same circles as the Gwynns.

Hall was having problems at home and was ready to give up racing. He was looking to unload a brand-new alcohol dragster and all the gear that went with it. Worried that he might lose the car in a pending divorce, that night he offered the complete package to Darrell and Jerry for $15,000.

"I pedaled my ass off," Darrell says. "I went home, all out of breath, and told my dad that Mr. Hall had a brand-new S&W dragster and all kinds of parts, and if we bring him $15,000, we can have it."

Jerry and Darrell went back to Hall's house, looked things over, and wrote the check that night. The sale included a fifth-wheel trailer, the race car, two Donovan engines, and a boatload of parts. The Gwynns, however, didn't run Donovans, so they called a couple of local guys and went to work selling some of the things they wouldn't use, including the trailer.

When all the dealing was done, the Gwynns had a brand-new alcohol dragster chassis in the garage and were in the black by about $25,000 or $30,000. They would use the profit to buy more familiar parts and later to get the chassis fitted for late-model engines.

While preparing the alcohol dragster, the team continued to race "Baby Huey". Despite only one car being ready to race, both machines made the trip to Bowling Green, Kentucky, for the annual Sportsnationals. At this national event, the alcohol dragsters and alcohol Funny Cars were the stars of the show—no Top Fuel, no nitro Funny Car,

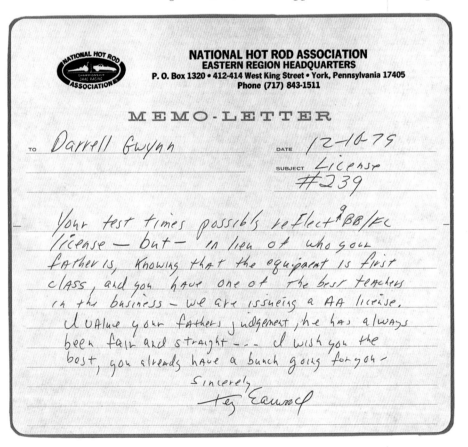

[38]

ABOVE: Jerry's reputation within the National Hot Rod Association helped ease the process of Darrell's getting a license. A letter from Terry Earwood reflects the sanctioning body's confidence in the young driver.
RIGHT: Miami-Hollywood Speedway Park time slips from Darrell's first NHRA licensing runs.

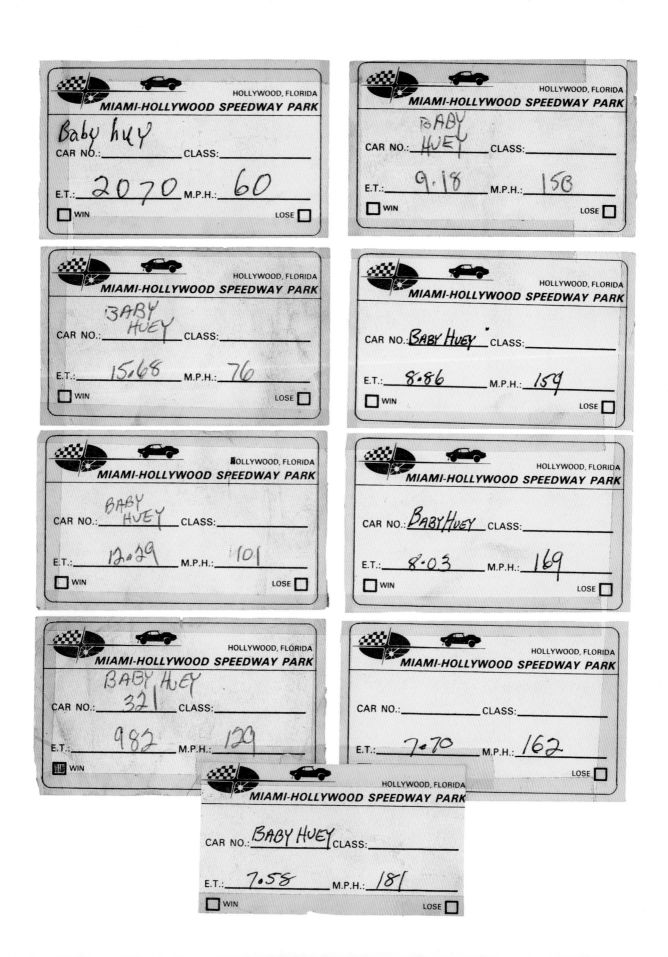

no Pro Stock.

"All the hot dogs from everywhere would go to the Sports-nationals," Darrell recalls. "It was the highest-paying race on the circuit for the alcohol cars. It was our premier event."

On the way to Bowling Green, however, Jerry injured his back trying to lift more than he could handle. He couldn't climb into the roadster, so the team turned to eighteen-year-old Darrell, who had run only small Florida points races at Bithlow and Bradenton. Jerry convinced NHRA director of competition Steve Gibbs to allow Darrell to fill in, despite the car being registered with Jerry listed as the driver.

Darrell qualified the AA Altered in the middle of the pack, but insisted it was on a great run and would have performed better had the parachutes not come out early.

He took the line for his first professional race in a national event against Joe Amato, who would go on to win five Top Fuel championships and become the winningest driver in Top Fuel history. Though he didn't score an upset against the future champ, Darrell says that under the circumstances he was more than pleased with his debut.

"At the end of the day, with thirty-five or forty cars there to qualify and it's Darrell Gwynn's first race, my first national event and I qualify twelfth," Darrell says. "Yeah, I went out first round, and yeah, I lost to Joe Amato, but they knew we were there. It was pretty cool."

Out in the parking lot, the new dragster sat on the back of an open trailer, waiting for a 750-mile, postrace trip to the S&W Race Cars chassis shop in Spring City, Pennsylvania, to be fitted for a 412-cubic-inch Chrysler Hemi engine. The coming days were to be a long, strange trip, complete with a van with a rhino painted on the side, some questionable vision, and a sign reading "Pollock Auto Museum"; life on the road provided never-ending stories for those back home.

"Dick 'Gunner' Clawson was hauling the alcohol dragster on an open trailer that we had borrowed," Darrell says. "He was towing it with a Ford van with a rhino painted on the side for God knows why, and we were off to Pennsylvania. We just thought it was best to get the car fitted by the people who did the original work. If we were going to do this, we were going to do it right.

"Gunner, who was half blind, stopped the van in the middle of the freeway at 2 A.M. to read the signs," Darrell adds. "I'm just sitting there thinking, 'Oh shit, we're gonna die.' Cars were passing us on both sides at 80 mph. I was thinking I'd never get to see my car race, because we were going to get rear-ended right here on the freeway."

Surviving the unscheduled pit stop, Gunner and Darrell rolled into Pottstown, Pennsylvania, where Darrell noticed a small sign

LEFT: The infamous "Rhino van" belonging to Dick "Gunner" Clawson. Gunner and Darrell traveled to Pennsylvania to get Darrell's first dragster fitted, collecting adventures along the way. The race car was towed behind on an open trailer. (Darrell Gwynn collection) **BELOW:** Darrell's first national event competition was in Bowling Green, Kentucky. He got behind the wheel at the Sportsnationals after Jerry injured his back. Darrell qualified well, but was eliminated in the first round by future five-time Top Fuel champ Joe Amato. (Les Welch)

ABOVE: Darrell takes on Indy in a dragster Jerry purchased from Miami neighbor Bob Hall. (Les Welch) **RIGHT:** *National Dragster* clipping from Indy.

"When we pulled the cover off the car in the morning, there were peanuts everywhere. And not just peanuts, but peanuts painted green. We were doomed."

reading "Pollock Auto Museum." Having some fun with pronunciation, Darrell couldn't resist. The mischievous pair stopped the Rhino van, fumbled through the toolbox for a 9/16 socket wrench, and began removing the bolts on the sign, later making it a permanent fixture at the family race shop in Florida.

As the dragster neared completion, Darrell would race the Altered for the team again later that year in Englishtown, New Jersey, but the story would be a little different than it had been in Bowling Green. After qualifying well and winning in the first round, the engine explosions began.

The team went to the race with two motors and blew up both of them in consecutive runs. In those days, it was unusual for alcohol motors to blow up even every one or two years, so the Gwynns went home to Florida wondering about their racing future. Despite Jerry's acknowledgement that his parts were "junk," Darrell thinks bad luck—caused by peanuts, long seen as a superstitious snack in car racing—had something to do with it.

"We were scheduled to race Gary Clark in the first round and his brother, Dave, left us a little gift," Darrell recalls. "When we pulled the cover off the car in the morning, there were peanuts everywhere. And not just peanuts, but peanuts painted green. We were doomed."

With two broken motors, the hobby racers with an all-volunteer crew were facing a seemingly insurmountable obstacle. It was definitely time to get the dragster sorted out, but Jerry and Darrell knew they needed a little help. They turned to racing standout and good friend Ken Veney for direction.

"We called up Veney and said, 'Look, we want to buy one or two sets of heads.

We are trying to put an alcohol dragster deal together, and we need help with an engine combination,'" Darrell says. Veney, who also raced alcohol Funny Cars and went on to race nitro Funny Cars, just happened to be in an alcohol dragster at the time and agreed to help the young operation.

"With the information Veney gave us, we took the car to Miami-Hollywood and made a couple of squirts down the track," Darrell says. "I think the best I ran was a 7.12, so what made us think we were ready for the U.S. Nationals I will never understand.

"But we knew we had some really good engine pieces that could possibly make us competitive. The day after testing, we left for Veney's shop in Wadsworth, Ohio, to make some test runs that he could watch at nearby Dragway 42. We couldn't even get down the racetrack, but we did manage to get some little things fixed."

The Gwynns worked next to Veney for the next few days, getting ready for the 1980 U.S. Nationals and the debut of Darrell's alcohol dragster.

At Indy, just a few days before his nineteenth birthday, Darrell

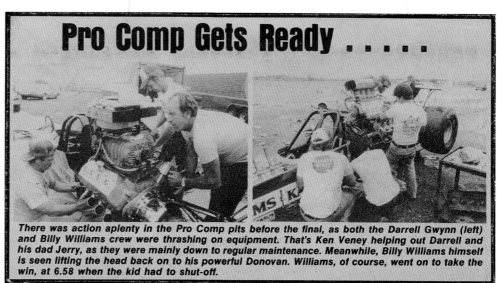

Pro Comp Gets Ready . . . . .

There was action aplenty in the Pro Comp pits before the final, as both the Darrell Gwynn (left) and Billy Williams crew were thrashing on equipment. That's Ken Veney helping out Darrell and his dad Jerry, as they were mainly down to regular maintenance. Meanwhile, Billy Williams himself is seen lifting the head back on to his powerful Donovan. Williams, of course, went on to take the win, at 6.58 when the kid had to shut-off.

"One of the coolest things I remember about my first final was all the guys I had sold clutch coolers to as a kid—Al Segrini, Don Prudhomme, Raymond Beadle, and 'Waterbed' Fred Miller—were up front cleaning the track off for me."

ABOVE: Darrell's first national event final occurred at drag racing's biggest event of the year—the U.S. Nationals. Darrell lost to Billy Williams. "He was one bad hombre," says Darrell. (Les Welch)

started with a run of 6.76. Then he ran a 6.70, before finally qualifying in the top half of the field with a 6.67.

"I was starting to get more comfortable in the car, and we knocked off a couple of the hot dogs on the way to the final," Darrell said. "This was when it was a 32-car Pro Comp field with five rounds of racing, not like the 16-car fields of today. In the finals, I was nervous as crap and we lost to Billy Williams. Billy was the best in the class that year. He was a bad hombre, but I helped him a lot by screwing up, over-revving the motor, and some other stupid things.

"One of the coolest things I remember about my first final was all the guys I had sold clutch coolers to as a kid—Al Segrini, Don Prudhomme, Raymond Beadle, and 'Waterbed' Fred Miller—were up front cleaning the track off for me. Waterbed Fred was kicking the rocks away, and I look over and Prudhomme's watching me. It was a very cool feeling."

With Darrell getting seat time in only a few more races in 1980, the Gwynns set their sights on 1981 and the possibility of running two cars—Darrell in the newly named Top Alcohol Dragster class

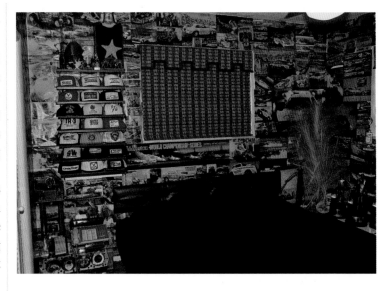

and Jerry in a new alcohol Funny Car. In preparation, the Gwynns spent $13,000 on a single-axle, cab-over-truck Peterbilt tractor and another $10,000 on an old moving trailer, and they built a rig to haul two race cars and a tow vehicle.

The plan was to open the season in Gainesville, and there still was a lot of work to be done. Family and friends thrashed to get the trailer customized and the two cars ready for the Gatornationals, working until midnight in the front yard before the team finally pulled away. With Jerry exhausted and Darrell not having a clue about driving a big rig, friend Gary Marjama got behind the wheel. Six hours later, the rig pulled into Gainesville Raceway and the road-weary team managed to grab an hour or so of sleep before the gates opened.

"We rolled in there and had 2 by 4 ramps to unload the Funny Car, and a lot of other makeshift stuff just to get ready for that event," Darrell recalls. "We had good parts and a lot of manpower, but not the kind of manpower that's on the payroll. We took 'em when we could get 'em."

ABOVE: Darrell celebrates with Chris and Michelle Cunningham in the Gwynn garage after his runner-up finish at Indy in 1980. (Darrell Gwynn collection) **ABOVE RIGHT:** Visitor's to Darrell's bedroom during his teenage years didn't have to think too long and hard about what Darrell's interests were. (Francis Butler, Darrell Gwynn collection)

Neither car stunned the field at the Gatornationals. Darrell qualified fifth at 6.648, 210.77 mph, before going out in the second round to number one qualifier and eventual race winner, Joe Amato. Jerry qualified last in an 11-car field, losing in the first round to Don Gerardot. It was a start, but Darrell had a lot to learn.

A Southeast Division points meet at Bradenton Motorsports Park proved pivotal to Darrell's growth as a driver. The alcohol dragster was running through the field until it reached the semifinals, when the parachutes failed and sent the car rolling over into a cornfield at the end of the 1/4 mile.

"I'm laying upside down in a cornfield and the whole season's ahead of me," Darrell says. "Shit, now what do I do? All these races ahead of me. It's supposed to be my big chance, and I've bent up the car and I'm trying my best to climb out of this wreck before my parents see me."

Uninjured, Darrell ignored ambulance workers and climbed out of the car, wanting to look unfazed when his parents came to pick him up. On the ride home, Jerry again offered Darrell the opportunity to walk away with no pressure, but Darrell decided he wanted to keep going.

If that was the case, it was time for Bradenton lesson number two—learning to drive the tractor trailer. In order for Jerry to keep his job and meet Darrell on the weekends, someone had to be responsible for moving the rig around the country between races.

"Dad asked me if I wanted to get the car fixed, and I said yes," Darrell says. "Then he told me that if I wanted it fixed, I was going to have to learn how to drive the truck so I could take the chassis back up to Pennsylvania to have it repaired. So the day I

Darrell Gwynn took a wild ride after his semi-final round win in Top Alcohol Dragster and bent up his race car a bit. Naturally, he was not able to return for the final, but once again a safely built race car came through and a driver walked away unhurt. **Photo by Marty Johnson**

crash my race car, still a little bit shaken, is the day I learn to drive a tractor trailer."

Darrell got his first taste of truck-driving school on Highway 27, a deadly two-lane Florida road commonly used in the early eighties by trucks hauling sugarcane. When they got home, Jerry knew just how much Darrell wanted to go racing.

"It was about four in the morning, and I heard all this noise outside and in the garage," Jerry recalls. "I walked out and Darrell was unloading the trailer and stripping the car, telling me he was leaving in the morning to go get it fixed."

A week later, the car was repaired and ready to go racing. But after the accident, something was different. A car that had been kicking ass just weeks before in Bradenton was now struggling, shaking and laboring to make it down the track.

Jerry's Funny Car, in the meantime, won the Cajun Nationals but didn't do much after that. It broke a lot of parts and found very little success, as the team spent most of its time developing the dragster.

Following the Springnationals in Columbus, Ohio, the team returned to Veney's nearby shop to try to figure out where the problem was with Darrell's dragster. The engine sounded strong, but the rear tires kept slipping. The team needed to find a way to get more weight distributed to the back of the car.

"We tried raising the front of the 412-cubic-inch Chrysler Hemi, changing the centerline of the crankshaft, and transferring more weight to the rear wheels," Darrell says. "While my dad stayed at Veney's shop and worked on the engines, I borrowed Veney's trailer to take the chassis to a shop in Cleveland and laid it out on the floor, finishing at about 3:30 in the morning. I drove it back to Veney's shop by myself, we loaded up the motor, and headed to Bowling Green for the Sportsnationals, showing up a day late."

The effects of the changes were immediate, as Darrell remembers the ride being "badass fast—a whole new race car."

Getting to the final after knocking off Amato in the semis, the

LEFT: *National Dragster* coverage of Darrell's crash in a Bradenton cornfield. **ABOVE:** In 1981, Darrell's first NHRA national event victory came at the venue where he made his national debut, the Sportsnationals in Bowling Green. That event was one of the sport's biggest in that era. More than sixty cars would enter and be whittled down to a field of sixteen. (Darrell Gwynn collection)

team turned to clutch specialist and friend Bob DeVour, who worked for Mr. Gasket at the racetrack.

"We pulled up for the final against Al DaPozzo, and DeVour comes over to the staging area and asked if we had left everything alone after running so well on the previous run. My dad told Bob that he had added another tooth of blower, but Bob convinced us that conditions were getting cooler and we should switch back to the way we had it."

Leaving the supercharger pulleys alone was the right call. Darrell, dressed in a raggedy old Jeb Allen T-shirt, went on to win the Sportsnationals, his first national event victory, collecting $14,000 in winnings at the division's biggest event of the year.

It was a proud moment for a team that was basically Jerry and Darrell and a lot of volunteer help. Darrell's high school buddy Barry Stevens helped drive the tractor trailer for meal money. Mike Cunningham, a family friend who had raced with Jerry in the sixties, would take time off from his job at Delta to fly to the races and help on weekends as a fabricator. Mike's son, Chris, would work on the engine and travel with Darrell during the summers and would later begin flying in on weekends after taking a job with U.S. Air. Everybody just pitched in when they could, offering to help with whatever needed to be done, but Jerry and Darrell carried much of the load.

Jerry recalls, "1981 nearly killed me. I was building the engines for two cars, the transmissions for two cars, and the rear ends for two cars. All of this while working a full-time job and traveling to the races only on the weekends. It got to be tough on me."

With Jerry at home during the week and Darrell driving the cars to the next race, much of Darrell's training was done over the phone. "It was the only way I could keep up with things," Jerry says. "I'd call him up, and we'd degree the camshaft over the phone or I'd walk him through this or that. At least that way, when I got to the track, some of the work would be done." Adds Darrell, "I don't know what made us think we could run a two-car team with no hired help."

Jerry Gwynn shares his joy with Mr. Gasket's Stan Gill (left) and Bob DeVour after son Darrell won the Top Alky Dragster crown. Gwynn himself won the Cajun Nationals Alky Funny Car title only a few weeks back.

After the Sportsnationals, the alcohol dragster continued to be a rocket ship. It won the Summernationals, knocking off Amato in the final. Darrell was even starting to grab the attention of the California racing community that he had dreamed about as a kid.

On a trip to Fremont, California, the only drivers in the field from the Southeast were Darrell and Bill Mullins, a driver from Pelham, Alabama, with a small-block Chevy engine. Both proved they were ready to run with the big dogs. The pair qualified number one and number two at the inaugural Golden Gate Nationals, with Darrell turning in consistent runs of 6.45, 6.42, and 6.41. He ultimately knocked off Mullins in the fastest alcohol dragster race in the sport's history, an eye-popping run of 6.41 at 214.28 mph to Mullins's 6.43 at 210.76 mph.

"We shut up the California boys big time," Darrell says. "They had been talking trash all year long, and they were waiting for us." A week later, Darrell backed up his performance with a runner-up finish at Orange County International Raceway. He made it clear to the entire drag racing community that they were dealing with a real player.

Chapter Four: The Road to a Championship

Though Darrell had convinced the drag racing community that he was more than capable behind the wheel by the age of twenty, not everyone was aware of Darrell's high-speed skills. While piloting the team hauler to Montreal in 1982 for a run in "Le Grandnationals," Darrell was stopped at the border.

"Here I am, a baby-faced twenty-something kid getting out of a semi, trying to convince a guy with a badge that I'm the one driving the rig," says Darrell, whose CB handle was "Big Red" after Winston gave the team a few thousand dollars to paint the Gwynn trailer crimson and carry the Winston Drag Racing lettering. "I've got my twenty-year-old girlfriend, Michelle Cunningham, with me and her little brother, Chris, who is probably about fifteen. It must have looked like a bunch of kids stole a truck and were trying to run off with it.

"We were pretty young to have that kind of responsibility," Darrell adds. "When I think back to what little street smarts you have at that age and to know we were driving down the road in the middle of the night in an 18-wheeler, it was an amazing adventure.

"I can't tell you how many times we pulled into a Union 76 truck stop. That was the deal. It was the middle of the night, you'd fill up with diesel, get a shower, wolf down a club sandwich, and hit the road again." But Darrell lived up to the responsibility, never putting even the smallest scratch on the 45-foot trailer in the nearly ten years he drove it.

On the track, the team continued to do well in 1982, winning two more national events, but for Darrell, driving the car was only part of the fun. In fact, most of the thrill came from simply being a part of the game.

"I was so into everything about that race team," Darrell says. "Barry Stevens, Chris, and I would stay up until all hours of the night, making sure all of the mechanical things were right, organizing everything we could, and trying to figure out what was going to get accomplished the next day. There was no time clock. We never looked up and said, 'Hey, it's five o'clock. Time to quit working.'"

And although it was always a safe bet that the best place to find Darrell was either behind the wheel of the team hauler or strapping in at the starting line, the gang did manage to squeeze in a bit of fun and frivolity along the way. And the boys didn't get into trouble all by themselves, running around in the early eighties with fellow racers like Don Woosley, Bubba Sewell, Al DaPozzo, and Bill Walsh.

As they worked their way through the NHRA's Sportsman classes, drag racers serious about winning championships tried to combine their best national events with their best regional points meets. The NHRA point system called for the best of both worlds. A critical part of the game was a little-white-lie strategy referred to as "blocking." With only a certain number of points meets required in one's own division, the trick was to move around the country and score at events where you stood the best chance of winning, often

LEFT: Darrell and Jerry side by side in 1982. (Darrell Gwynn collection)
ABOVE: The Division II banquet with director and family pal Lex Dudas (right). (Marty Johnson, courtesy Darrell Gwynn collection)

ABOVE: Jerry Gwynn took this 1977 Kentucky trailer and turned it into the team hauler, making the Gwynns one of the few alcohol teams to have such a luxury. Proof positive of Jerry's favorite saying: "If it can be built, I can build it." Before (Darrell Gwynn collection), after (John Powanda, Darrell Gwynn collection)

while attempting to misdirect your competition. The phone conversations would go something like this:

Darrell: "So, where are you guys heading this week?"

Bubba: "Oh, we're going up to Epping, New Hampshire—really looking forward to it."

Darrell: "Hey, me too. I'll see you there. Maybe we can grab a bite Friday night."

Two days later, Darrell would pull his rig into Amarillo, Texas, hoping Bubba had really gone on to New Hampshire. More times than not, however, they all pulled up to the same gate.

"Drivers are crazy," Jerry says. "They'll do anything to win a championship—even if it only pays $10."

The fun and camaraderie between Sportsman drivers extended well beyond the racetrack, with practical jokes and schoolboy antics filling time between 1/4-mile battles.

During downtime in Amarillo, Darrell, Brian Raymer, Buddy Domingue, and Bubba were enjoying dinner at the Big Texan, "Home of the 72-Ounce Steak." Strolling guitar and banjo musicians were making their rounds, playing for tips, when Darrell decided to have

a little fun with his friends, who were sitting at various tables.

"I was scheduled to race Raymer in the first round the next day, so I dedicated John Denver's 'Take Me Home Country Road' to him, letting him know what I thought of his chances of beating me and that he should just go on back to Denver where he was from," Darrell says with a laugh.

"For Sewell, I sent them over to sing 'Your Cheatin' Heart,' because even though he never cheated, his car always had an odd engine-weight combination and people used to kid him about bending the rules.

"And then over to Buddy Domingue's table to sing 'Born to Lose,' because he had one of the fastest cars out there every week, but he couldn't seem to win a race."

Darrell looks back fondly on friendships he made during those early years on the road. "Back then, we would pit together, drive down the road together, eat together, and laugh together," Darrell recalls. "It was a good time in racing. And every year I've been in racing since, a little bit of fun has been taken out of it. Just a little bit. But every year, it feels like we've lost a little more."

They had been competitive on the track in 1982, and for 1983, Darrell and Jerry prepared for a championship run, buying a lighter Bob Jinkins chassis, built in, of all places, a New Jersey chicken coop. The team set an aggressive event schedule, taking advantage of every opportunity to collect as many early points as possible.

And it would be Sewell, Darrell's close friend and competitor, who would help Darrell kick off the '83 campaign.

The Texas racer had no plans to run the season opener in Pomona. Darrell was planning to make the cross-country trip alone, so he asked

Sewell to join him in the 18-wheeler and help him at the race.

"Here's a guy I would ultimately be racing against for Winston championship points, helping me at the Winternationals," Gwynn said. "I picked him up at his house in Spring, Texas, sometime after midnight, he helped me drive the truck and helped me work on the car like it was his own. It was the way we did things back then."

Although Darrell had to settle for a runner-up finish in Pomona, the new car was lightning fast a few weeks later at Gainesville, running a 6.36 and covering a field that was running closer to 6.45. But an all-but-imperceptible mechanical problem would cost him the race. The team was using a funnel made from a section of radiator hose to transfer fuel into the hard-to-reach fuel tank. Each time the hose was dipped into the tank, it was losing tiny pieces of rubber against a vent edge.

By the time Darrell was ready to run the first round, two or three fuel-injector nozzles were clogged with the rubber fragments. With computers not making their way to the track until years later,

the problem was nearly impossible to detect until it was too late. The result was a destroyed blower and a major disappointment for the team, not to mention the Gainesville Raceway spectator bleachers stocked with Darrell's family and friends.

After the setback, the team—Darrell, Jerry, Mike and Chris Cunningham, and Gary Marjama—rebounded quickly, virtually clinching the Top Alcohol title by July, three months before the end of the season.

"Darrell was so focused on racing that he didn't pay attention to other things," Chris Cunningham says. "We were driving down the road and saw a sign for an antique store and Darrell asks 'What's an antique?' You just couldn't talk to him about anything else going on in the world that wasn't about racing."

Adding to the special year was a victory at Indy over Don Devault. But despite winning the U.S. Nationals and the alcohol dragster points title, Darrell knew he wanted to do more behind the wheel.

"We had accomplished our number one priority for the season,"

ABOVE: Darrell always made time for fishing despite his busy racing schedule. "Catching that 40-pound amberjack felt like I was pulling up a Volkswagen," he says. (Darrell Gwynn collection) **TOP RIGHT:** Good friend and crafty competitor Bubba Sewell helps Darrell work on his car at the Winternationals in 1983. "That's just the way it was back then. Even though we raced against each other, we still helped each other out," Darrell recalls. (Darrell Gwynn collection)

"Back then, we would pit together, drive down the road together, eat together, and laugh together," Darrell recalls. "It was a good time in racing."

ABOVE: Darrell, still dressed in his fire suit, shoots baskets with R. J. Reynolds's representative Jeff Byrd. The basketball setup was another of Jerry's homemade gadgets, folding out from the back door of the trailer. "Things are a little more serious at the track these days," Darrell observes. (Darrell Gwynn collection)

LEFT: Friends of the family hung this banner across the street from Darrell's home. "I'll never forget turning the corner and seeing this sign," Darrell says. "You could see it from I-95." (Darrell Gwynn collection) **BELOW:** Team members made Darrell this "No Red Lights" T-shirt after he continued to have problems leaving the starting line early. (Darrell Gwynn collection) **RIGHT:** A *National Dragster* clipping from the Indy win.

"No Red Lights."

"My family members were calling me quicker than electricity, but everyone else was calling me a no-drivin' son-of-a-bitch," Darrell recalls. "There were numerous times when we were the number one qualifier, and I'd red-light in the first round. We couldn't figure out what was going on. We were lucky we clinched so early because it was becoming a real problem."

Despite the red-light headaches, the team enjoyed every minute of the '83 season, often looking for ways to relax as the year wore on. Going for the Winston championship meant a lot of extra time on the road, so Darrell and the crew made sure to bring along the necessities.

Darrell says. "However, without sounding too cocky, we expected to win the championship with the effort we were putting forth. It wasn't about money. It was about having all the right pieces, having the right group of people together, making the right decisions, and having a lot of luck. Most of those things money can't buy.

"I was thrilled with winning the championship and it was great for all the people who had been supporting us, but part of me was looking at it as nothing more than a credential builder for Top Fuel," Darrell adds. "I was already thinking about moving on."

With the championship in the bag by July, the team spent the remainder of the season tinkering with the car and trying to figure out why Darrell was seeing as many red lights as green at the starting line. He would jump the start nearly a dozen times before season's end. At the Orange County race, the team became so fed up with Darrell that they had T-shirts printed with a Christmas tree in the middle of a red circle and a line through it. Underneath were written the words

A very pleased Jerry Gwynn embraces son, <u>Darrell</u>, after his young charge took the coveted Alcohol Dragster title at Indy. The Gwynn's dragster ran strong all weekend long.

"I always seemed to have a girlfriend with me, and my fishing pole was never far away," Darrell laughs. "And we all liked to play a little basketball, so Dad came up with one of his gadgets, connecting a backboard and hoop on a hinge to the back door of the trailer. We'd fold it up, put a pin in it, and the games would begin. The Glidden family, Bob, Billy, and Rusty, and Rich Habegger from Winston were regulars when we broke out the basketball. Between that and constantly being on the lookout for a nearby pond or fishing hole, we had a lot of fun."

At Columbus in 1983, the concept "girlfriend" took on new significance as Darrell noticed the daughter of Pennsylvania race team owner Bill Stanton sitting atop the family camper. In fact, he did a little more than notice—he walked by the area "about fifty times" hoping to catch Shelly's eye.

When Darrell discovered that his old friend Donnie Irvan was driving for Stanton, he asked his buddy to make the introduction. Darrell and Shelly went out that weekend and a week later, Darrell visited the Stantons at their Ferrell, Pennsylvania, home.

The two went on to date for several years, with Shelly helping out where she could with the race team. "Shelly was on the road with us nearly the whole time," Darrell says. "She ran errands, made sandwiches, and took care of a lot of things that really helped the team. It may not sound like a lot, but she was a big help."

Coming back to defend his Winston title in 1984, Darrell and Shelly were joined on the road by Darrell's high school friend Dave Tomasch. The team tried to repeat the formula that had worked so well in 1983.

The season got off to an uncomfortable start—for Shelly. They had skipped Pomona, so the national event season for the Gwynn team opened in Gainesville. There, Darrell lined up in the final against Bill Stanton's car, with Irvan behind the wheel. Shelly, conflicted as to which car to stand behind, ended up standing in the center between the two cars, with Darrell going on to win the race. Problem solved.

Darrell's problems with red-lighting continued as the '84 season wore on. Worse still was the threat posed by a Division I driver named Bill Walsh, who stood between Darrell and his quest for back-to-back titles.

"He just wore us out," Darrell says. "He was always a tick better. I'd leave on him and he'd drive around me and beat me by a foot. It seemed like our cars would change positions several times down the track, but he'd always seem to get us at the end. He had a mean, mean car."

On his way to Brainerd, however, Darrell made a wise decision, stopping at Don Garlits's Ocala, Florida, race shop in search of answers. After Darrell explained the red-lighting problems he was having at the line, he backed the car into Big Daddy's museum and removed all the panels. Garlits jacked the car up, slid a 6 by 6 piece of railroad tie under the driver's compartment, and began schooling the young driver in chassis dynamics.

Garlits began jumping up and down on the front of the skinned car. Every time he jumped, the rear wheels began to come off the

ABOVE: Darrell with Mr. Gasket's Bob DeVour. "I owe a lot of my early success to Bob," Darrell says. "We raced hard together and we played hard together." (Darrell Gwynn collection) **RIGHT:** Victory lane at the 1983 U.S. Nationals. (Whit Bazemore, courtesy Darrell Gwynn collection)

Summers on the Road

Hanging out with racing friends over the summers, Darrell spent as much time with Carl Ruth, Ralph Gorr, Don Ness, Ken Veney, and the Clark family as he did at home in Miami.

"Ten years straight, I stayed at Carl Ruth's house in Pennsylvania around the Reading race," Darrell says with a laugh. "When I was in the Ohio area, I stayed at the Veney's house, and Ralph's house in Mission Viejo was our California bachelor pad, so you can imagine some of the stories from that place. And we won't even talk about Don's place in Minnesota.

"Ken, who was one of the best drag racers of his era, spent a lot of time schooling me in my early days, and some of the sacrifices the Veneys made when I was visiting were amazing," Darrell adds. "I'd eat dinner with them and have dessert and then sit and wait while they watched TV on the couch that was also my bed.

"The only downstairs bathroom in the house was through their bedroom, so if I'd get up in the middle of the night to go to the bathroom, I'd have to parade through their bedroom. And I was staying there for weeks at a time."

While he was visiting Gorr in Mission Viejo, the pair decided it was time for a party. With no female friends around, it was time to improvise.

Stretching a piece of yellow tape used to mark off a racer's pit area across the road in front of Gorr's house, Darrell and Ralph attempted to stop cars in search of good-looking women. They were coming up dry until a white Porsche with a bumper sticker reading "No Tiny Weenies" pulled to a stop.

"We couldn't believe it," Darrell recalls. "Three beautiful California girls jump out and spend the evening having a blast with us at Ralph's house. By five o'clock they were dancing on the tables."

Carl Ruth, a Pennsylvania drag racer, met Darrell through Jerry.

Ruth, who claims he "felt sorry" for Jerry and Darrell at a race in Gainesville after the pair had blown up just about everything in sight, jokingly offered to "straighten Darrell up" back at his Pennsylvania garage.

Jerry wasn't laughing and happily sent young Darrell to Ruth's place when the team was racing in the Northeast.

The pair forged a strong bond, spending a lot of time hanging out at Mom's Diner, where Darrell often introduced Ruth as his "second dad." To this day, a sign declaring an upstairs bedroom "Darrell's Den" still hangs in Ruth's house.

Darrell says he learned a lot about racing working shoulder to shoulder with Ruth in an eight-car garage located in the shadows of Maple Grove Raceway. But most of Ruth's memories are a little more explosive.

"There used to be a break between Englishtown and the race at Sanair," Ruth says. "The break fell around the Fourth of July, so a lot of the racers would come over to my place to set off some fireworks and drink some beer."

OK, this wasn't sparklers and firecrackers: thousands of dollars were spent loading an 8-foot pickup bed to the top with anything that might burst into flames or make a lot of noise. These guys were used to working with alcohol and nitro for a living, so the explosions had to be spectacular.

Whether it was blowing up gas cans with dynamite, shooting pistons across the lake at Englishtown, or flipping cars with black powder, nothing topped loading a 55-gallon drum with a gallon of gasoline, a gallon of nitro, and a waxed stick of dynamite with a long cigarette fuse that Darrell helped construct.

"We went back up to Carl's roof and watched through binoculars as the fuse burned down," Darrell remembers. "When that thing went off, the top flew so high we couldn't see it and the bottom opened up like a birdbath." The Independence Day carnage included the total destruction of nearly a dozen innocent pine trees.

On the track, Darrell and his "second dad" shared some special memories as well.

"In 1982, there used to be a summer race in Reading called the Budweiser Super Stock Nationals," Darrell recalls. "It was a big deal for Carl because it was his hometown race, and we both went out and won that event. It was one of Carl's biggest wins in his career, and it was very cool to share that moment with him."

Says Ruth: "I never had any children, so I really consider Darrell to be my son. I've watched him grow from the kid who would walk around polishing wheels for 50 cents apiece into a man who inspires everyone he meets. I'm very proud to know Darrell Gwynn."

ground. The car was too stiff. The front tires were lifting out of the timing beam, giving the illusion that the car had left the starting line, triggering the red light.

Garlits's solution was to remove the diagonal frame tubes from the center of the chassis to allow more flex in the frame and keep the front wheels in the beam until they moved forward. They ran cables from the driver's compartment under the car and back up toward the front wheel. Now, the car would arch in the right spot and the cables would keep it from sagging once it came down.

The process was tested after each set of diagonals was removed from the foot box forward. Garlits kept jumping on the front of the car until he got the flex he wanted.

"Here's my beautiful Bob Jinkins car and we're cutting it all up," Darrell says. "I'm a little worried, but I'm sitting there watching Big Daddy work on my car, so I'm certainly confident. When he cut the third set out and bounced, he said 'Now, we're talking.'"

The Garlits modifications worked, and Darrell went on to win the event at Brainerd. But although he went on to earn a second divi-

sional championship, the chassis fix came too late to catch Walsh for the Winston title.

With ten national event wins under his belt, however, Darrell felt like it was time to make the jump to the nitromethane-burning cars of Top Fuel. "By the end of 1984, the team was losing a little bit of motivation," Darrell says. "We had accomplished so much so fast in the alcohol car, and I knew Top Fuel was where I needed to be if I was going to make a living driving a car. We were confident we could be competitive, and that made us believe we were ready to make the jump."

Darrell found a buyer for his alcohol dragster and some of the team's motors. By the end of the season, a friend of Darrell's was hauling the car to California to close the deal and came home with about $90,000.

"I was like Frosted Flakes without the milk," Darrell recalls.

ABOVE: The 1983 NHRA Winston championship banquet table. (Darrell Gwynn collection) **ABOVE RIGHT:** A thank-you note in *National Dragster* from Darrell to his supporters.

"I was a driver with no car, so it was time to either go for it in Top Fuel or quit racing. After talking with my parents, we decided we couldn't afford it, but we went for it anyway. I was young and dumb, and somehow or another I was going to be a Top Fuel racer who made money."

The first step was gathering information.

"I called fuel system specialist and good friend Ralph Gorr and gave him a laundry list of about $5,000 worth of parts I needed," Darrell says. "Ralph called back and said he'd take care of all of it—fuel pumps, injectors, lines, barrel valves, you name it. And it seemed like no matter who I called, I got the same kind of response. I was overwhelmed with the way people reacted to the requests. I had a lot of decals on the car that year, and I realized that it was all those deals that meant so much and kept us at the racetrack. It's those donated products and cut-rate deals that helped us survive on a shoestring budget."

With an endless list of Top Fuel parts he needed to secure, Darrell put in calls to two of drag racing's top chassis makers, Al Swindahl and Davey Uyehara. He gave them both every sob story he could think of to persuade them to stay within his budget. Swindahl came back with a price tag between $26,000 and $28,000—Darrell needed it to be closer to $14,000.

TOP: "That just says it all," Darrell observes of the decal on the wing of his race car. (Darrell Gwynn collection) ABOVE: At the 1984 Gatornationals final, Darrell raced friend Donnie Irvin, who was piloting a car owned by Bill Stanton, the father of Darrell's girlfriend Shelly. (Auto Imagery)

"I was like Frosted Flakes without the milk," Darrell recalls. "I was a driver with no car, so it was time to either go for it in Top Fuel or quit racing."

Darrell thought he was finished. Then he got a second call. Uyehara, who built cars for Frank Bradley, Dick LaHaie, and a lot of other West Coast drivers, came in at $13,600 with one condition: Darrell would have to make himself available to come out to Uyehara's California shop and help work on it.

"Now the program was coming together," Darrell recalls. "Ralph was taking care of the fuel system, we worked a deal for some cylinder heads with Veney, and now Davey Uyehara was giving us a price we could work with on the chassis."

In December 1984, Darrell was encouraged by friend and part-time advisor Bob Abdellah to make the trip to nearby Palm Beach for the Citrus Nationals. Abdellah knew that Garlits would be match racing at the event, and his idea was to have a public relations photo taken with Big Daddy welcoming young Darrell to the Top Fuel ranks. The "come on in, the water's fine" photo was an immediate hit, especially with the hometown Florida media.

"I knew Darrell was going to get off to a good start," Garlits recalls. "He had a good background, spending all those years with Jerry.

Coming from a racing family is a big plus, and racing with the support of your family is an even bigger plus.

"And Darrell always wanted to learn," Garlits adds. "Even when he was a kid hanging around the pits, he didn't talk a lot and he soaked it all in. You could tell even then that he wanted to be a racer."

Darrell continued to gather helpful information at Palm Beach. It would be one of his old clutch cooler customers who came through with a treasure chest of Top Fuel contacts and phone numbers.

"Dad and I were hanging out at Raymond Beadle's trailer with Dale Emery, Dee Gant, and Waterbed Fred," Darrell recalls. "Raymond opened his Rolodex and just by asking a few questions about who we should see about certain things, Raymond started rattling off contacts. He opened every page and gave us all he had."

With plans to start the 1985 racing year in Gainesville, Darrell traveled to the season opener in Pomona. He picked up the Uyehara chassis in Yuba City and also made the rounds to collect motors, blowers, magnetos, and anything else he ordered from West Coast suppliers.

ABOVE: Darrell and his former girlfriend Shelly Stanton. (Darrell Gwynn collection) **RIGHT:** In victory lane following the 1984 Gatornationals. From left to right: Gene Kidder, Gary Marjama, John Wright, Joan, Jerry, Becky Marshall, Darrell, Shelly Stanton, Chris Cunningham, and Joe Shaffer. (Whit Bazemore, Darrell Gwynn collection)

"I remember driving all over the state of California to pick up parts," Darrell says. "But what I remember even more is the enthusiasm everyone showed for our team when I stopped in. I'd hear 'We got you two good blowers there, young man,' or 'We got you the two best mags [magnetos that spark the engine] that ever came out of here.' These are all people I had done business with before, and they knew we were taking a risk and they were excited for us."

As Darrell rounded up his parts and pieces, there was still one element that could have become a deal breaker. His crew, still all volunteer, could have asked for a paycheck. "That would have killed us," Darrell admits. "If the guys had said 'Hey, we're going Top Fuel racing and we want $500 a week,' it would have died right there."

But the crew—Mike and Chris Cunningham, Dave Tomasch, Joe Schaffer, and Andre Hayes—enthusiastically stayed on for the ride. "I can honestly say that I would have never gotten as far as I did in racing without the Cunninghams," Darrell says. "Without their sacrifice, we never could have moved on."

"We didn't get paid until Darrell's second year of Top Fuel and even then it was peanuts, maybe $50 a race," Chris Cunningham says. "But it wasn't about money back then. It was about the satis-

faction of beating the teams that did have money and earning the respect of the people you raced with every weekend. It was about more than money."

Just as things were falling into place for a legitimate Top Fuel effort, a smaller event took place at home in 1984 that would ultimately be a turning point in Darrell's life. Family friend Ronnie Hughes pulled into the Gwynn driveway in a new Camaro with his eighteen-year-old niece, Lisa Hurst. The car was Lisa's high school graduation present, and Ronnie was hoping Darrell could set her up with some car care products he had gathered over the years from his sponsors.

Darrell and Lisa certainly weren't strangers; they had shared family holidays and weekend trips together as children, but they were five years apart in age and Darrell remembered little more than the "skits and dances" Lisa would put on to entertain the family at Thanksgiving dinner.

Uncle Ronnie's true intentions, however, were fairly transparent. He was hoping sparks would fly. Ronnie tried many times to bring the pair together, even going as far as putting racing tapes of Darrell

LEFT: As the saying goes, the apple doesn't fall far from the tree. "I'm not sure what happened on this day," Darrell says, "but I doubt we won the race." (Darrell Gwynn collection) **ABOVE:** Darrell at age fourteen, with family friends Michelle (six) and Lisa Hurst (nine) on vacation at Disney World. Little did they know that Lisa and Darrell would wed many years later. (Darrell Gwynn collection)

in the VCR when Lisa's boyfriends were visiting. Darrell's mother, Joan, and Ronnie's wife, Diane, were best friends and coconspirators in the effort, with a little push here and there and a lot of cheerleading behind the scenes.

"Her aunt and I would get together and get so excited about the possibility of the two of them getting together," Joan admits. "I'd always

politely ask Darrell about his girlfriend, but I always made sure to ask him about Lisa too." Although Darrell and Shelly Stanton were still together, and the car care package didn't exactly lead to a love connection that afternoon, the interest had been ignited on Darrell's part. Over the next few years, he often asked about Lisa.

[65]

Chapter Five:
Breathin' Nitro

Darrell's Top Fuel career opened with a bang—a very loud bang.

At the team's request, veteran nitro crew chief Bill Schultz joined the Gwynns in West Palm Beach at Florida's Moroso Motorsports Park. It was a few weeks before the 1985 Gatornationals, and they were hoping to get the fledgling Top Fuel unit ready to race. The first day of consultation was spent going over the basics, firing the car, and learning the tricks to warming a 3,500-horsepower engine.

Overnight, the car was left on a steep ramp in the trailer. The fuel lines were never disconnected and fuel flowed freely into the combustion chamber. The next morning, they cranked up the engine and ignited the fuel in the cylinders, blowing the engine to pieces.

"With the fuel tank a little higher than the injector, it pressurized the system," Jerry explains. "A little bit of fuel got through a barrel valve, and everyone knows that fuel in the cylinders is a no-no."

Thankfully, no one was injured, but the second day was spent repairing the damage and putting things back together. They delayed making the necessary licensing run until parts could be found. Finally, Darrell got to make a few test passes at Moroso.

"The feeling of a Top Fuel car compared to an alcohol car was totally different," Darrell says. "I was running as fast at half-track as the alcohol car was running at the finish line. The noise. The power. It's just a totally different animal."

As testing went on, friends of the Gwynn family wandered by, often offering contributions to the hometown operation.

"One of our friends asked how we were going to get tires," Darrell says. "I told him we'd have to get them when we got to the race and that they were about $400 a set. He gave us $1,400 and told us it was for tires. I guess we were carrying the flag for South Florida and everyone wanted to see us do well."

After earning his Top Fuel license at Moroso, Darrell and the team left West Palm Beach with shaky confidence. They had learned just enough to know they had a lot more to learn.

At Gainesville, the car ran in the 5.80s in its Top Fuel debut, qualifying Darrell in the middle of the pack for the Gatornationals. Despite falling in the first round to Gary Ormsby, Darrell and the team felt like they were on the right track.

The car continued to be competitive in 1985, qualifying for every race, scoring runner-up finishes to Garlits at Englishtown and Indy, and qualifying as high as first at the season finale at the World Finals in Pomona, where Darrell defeated former NFL quarterback Dan Pastorini before falling to Gene Snow in the second round.

"Being at Indy against Garlits in the final was big," Darrell says. "We had an oil line come off about a hundred feet off the starting line. We have a picture in my shop of the oil line just as it was coming off and we were ahead of him. Oil was spraying all over the place at 250 mph. We got in it and smoked the tires." The final result—Big Daddy collected his seventh Indy title with a 5.57 at 260.56 to Darrell's 5.75 at 250.13.

As Darrell sits remembering that day, a smile comes over his

LEFT: Darrell blocks the sun with his hand as he waits in the staging area at Pomona. (Mark Mezzano, Darrell Gwynn collection) **ABOVE:** Darrell gets fitted for the new chassis in the Gwynn race shop, in preparation for his first season of NHRA Top Fuel racing. (Darrell Gwynn collection)

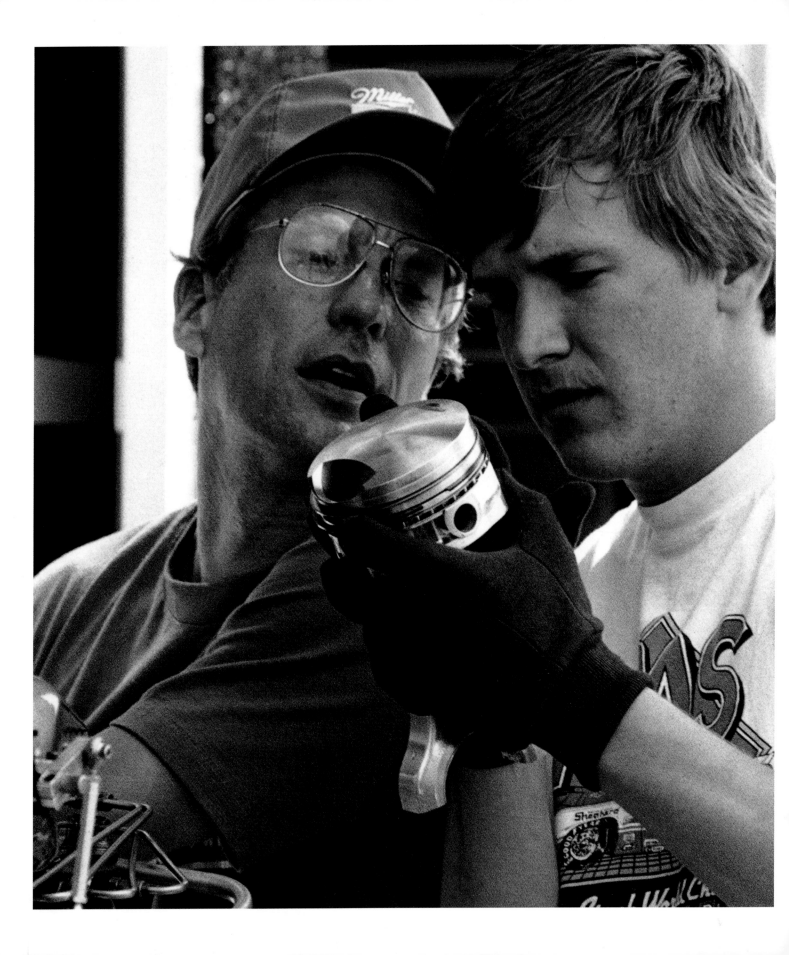

face. "His ass was grass," he says with confidence. "We had it in our hands—we were so hurt."

A *National Dragster* article quoted Garlits after the race: "He's just getting started in this thing. Sort of like paying his college tuition. But he's going to race, who knows, another twenty-five years, and he's going to win a lot of these races. Trust me."

Matching up against Garlits, the man he idolized as a child, always meant a lot to Darrell, but it meant a lot to Big Daddy as well. "When Darrell was in the other lane, I tried really hard to think of him as just another racer, but he was like family to me," says Garlits, who nicknamed Darrell "the Wolf" after a Wolf Racing Products logo reminded him of the hungry young driver. "He was a special kid. He could have been the poster boy for American youth—tall, good-looking, well-mannered. If any father ever wished for a son, he'd have wished for one like Darrell Gwynn."

After Indy, the Gwynns' car really started to fly. The competition began to take notice, and the team had built a great foundation of information to study during the off-season. Darrell and the crew kept it simple, taking the car completely apart. They fine-tuned everything they could and searched for every possible way to reduce the car's weight.

In 1986, the team returned to Pomona for the Winternationals,

FIRST LOOK!!!—GWYNN'S NEW FUELER

Darrell "the Kid" Gwynn was out testing his new Top Fueler at Moroso Motorsports Park in southern Florida the weekend before the Gatornationals. Darrell never made a full run in the Dave Uyehara-built racer, but did tell DRAGSTER that "Horsepower isn't gonna be a problem!!"

March 22, 1985—National DRAGSTER—Page 5

Brad Fedlin

LEFT: Darrell and Jerry turned to veteran nitro crew chief and friend Bill Schultz for advice as the team prepared to make the move to Top Fuel. "We learned just enough to know we had a lot more to learn," Darrell says. (Peter Tritley, Darrell Gwynn collection) **ABOVE:** *A National Dragster* clipping of Darrell's new Top Fuel car.

ABOVE: Darrell prepares for the first round against Gary Ormsby at the Gatornationals, the Gwynns' first Top Fuel event. (Darrell Gwynn collection) **TOP RIGHT:** Darrell inspects a destroyed piston, trying to determine the cause of the failure. Of the riddle of examining damaged parts from a blown engine, Darrell says, "It's like trying to decide which came first: the chicken or the egg." (Darrell Gwynn collection) **RIGHT:** Tony Mills at the wheel of the team's '73 Peterbilt gives Darrell a chance to rest on the way to the next event. (Darrell Gwynn collection) **FAR RIGHT:** Jerry gives Darrell the signature handshake at a race in 1985. (Les Welch)

starting the season in the same place they had finished so strongly the year before. Darrell qualified fourth in his unpainted hot rod, knocking off Jimmy King and Frank Bradley before running into Garlits again. This time, Darrell caught a break as Big Daddy broke an input shaft, while Darrell's run of 5.45 at 256 mph pushed him into a final-round matchup with Connie Kalitta.

In the final, both drivers cut a .497 light with Darrell turning the 1/4 mile in 5.46 at 257.87 to Kalitta's 5.72 at 209.79. The Kid—as he was labeled by Dave Clark, brother of Gwynn crew member Gary Clark—had scored his first Top Fuel victory.

"We had done the right thing in not changing too much from 1985, because the car was the most consistent it had ever been," Darrell recalls. "I hate to make it sound so easy, but we knew we could come back to Pomona and win that race. The car was easy to tune all weekend. I remember adjusting the clutch with the slightest of

weight, using just washers—and that car would respond."

The celebration in the winner's circle lasted for hours, with photo requests going on forever. Darrell tried to take individual photos with all the people who had helped him over the years. "It was their time to enjoy this," Darrell says. "These were the people who had helped us get where we were. These are the people that believed in Darrell Gwynn."

But Darrell's moment of victory would be short-lived. The program went downhill fast over the next few races, with the team blowing up everything in sight over the next four events. At one point, Darrell and Jerry even considered parking the car.

Back at home, the team took the car to Miami-Hollywood in an attempt to solve the riddle of why it continued to eat itself alive. "We changed everything trying to get it figured out," Darrell says. "We

just couldn't keep it together. It wanted to blow up every time we went down the track."

Through trial and error, the team eventually zeroed in on the supercharger as the likely source of the problem. Darrell called Gene Mooneyham, of Mooneyham Blowers in California, in search of a new blower that was available for next-day delivery. Mooneyham got the job done, piecing together a supercharger from parts he had in his shop.

The next day, Darrell fired the car up and hit the gas. "It was a totally different race car," Darrell recalls. "We knew right away we had found the problem. It lit on all eight cylinders, and the new blower really brought it to life."

And the car would get even better after conversations with longtime family friend Dale Armstrong, who was tuning the Budweiser Funny Car of Kenny Bernstein at the time. Armstrong had put together a dominant Funny Car engine combination and was

LEFT: At the 1986 Winternationals in Pomona, California, Darrell scored his first Top Fuel victory with a win against Connie Kalitta. (Auto Imagery)
ABOVE: Victory lane at Pomona. From left: Chris Cunningham, Mike Cunningham, Dave Tomash, Andre Hayes, Joe Shaffer, Joan, Jerry, Darrell, Shelly Stanton, and Tony Mills. (Auto Imagery)

"When I hit the gas, I looked over and saw Kenny standing about a hundred feet away and his eyes were wide open," Darrell says. "I'm sure mine were too. That car let out the biggest roar I had ever heard. It was so much fun. We couldn't wait to get that car to the finish line. We knew it was going to turn the world over, setting record after record."

The next race was in Montreal, where Darrell qualified number one, knocking off Pastorini, Amato, Garlits, and Dick LaHaie. Word was out and the crowds around Darrell's pit area began to grow. The Bernstein-Armstrong combination turned the Gwynns' Top Fuel ride into the dominant car on the circuit, winning the following race at Englishtown and qualifying number one at seven consecutive events.

"There is no one thing to point at that tells people why this combination was better than others," Jerry says. "It was the camshafts, the cam timing—it was everything working well together, making the car run smoother and with much more power."

"This car was just big-time fast," Darrell adds. "All you had to do was try to control this animal and you would win the race."

curious about what it could do in a dragster. At the Budweiser Superstock Nationals in Maple Grove, Pennsylvania, where Bernstein had to appear for his sponsor, they decided to give it a shot in Darrell's car in a test session after the race.

"Back in 1980, when I first started racing the Budweiser Funny Car, we were really struggling one afternoon at an event in Suffolk, Virginia," Bernstein recalls. "It was just me and a couple of guys in the beginning, and we really didn't have a crew chief. Jerry Gwynn, who didn't know me from any other racer out there, worked into the middle of the night one night to help us degree a camshaft.

"In addition to working on his own car, he took the time to help us out and I never forgot that," Bernstein adds. "We probably would have helped them anyway, but I always remembered that night in Virginia. Jerry Gwynn is one of the nicest people I know."

So, the new engine combination was set up in Darrell's car, and with dragsters using shorter headers than Funny Cars, the machine sounded that much stronger.

LEFT: "1990 was our year," Darrell says. "We were as confident as you could get and the intensity level was at an all-time high." (NHRA)
ABOVE: Chris Cunningham, Tony Mills, Andre Hayes, Joe Shaffer, and Dave Tomash doing the "Gwynn Shuffle" after winning at Pomona. (Darrell Gwynn collection) RIGHT: Darrell defeated Dick LaHaie to win the prestigious U.S. Nationals. "What a weekend," Darrell recalls. "We qualified number one, became the seventh member of the four-second club, set the national ET record, and won the race." (Wayne Ulmer)

TOP: Dale Armstrong and Darrell have birthdays within days of each other. At the U.S. Nationals, the team surprised the pair with a little pit-side entertainment. (Darrell Gwynn collection) **ABOVE:** In the Dallas tower Kenny Bernstein and Darrell prepare to announce that the two would be teammates under the Budweiser banner beginning in 1987. (Bob Abdellah) **TOP RIGHT:** In the winner's circle with the late Robert Goodwin and his daughter Robin. "Robert was a great friend," remembers Darrell. (Les Welch) **BOTTOM RIGHT:** Darrell sits behind the wheel of his brand new Budweiser Top Fuel dragster for the first time. The car proved to be too heavy. "We went back to Steve Davis's shop and took about 150 pounds off it," Darrell says. (Gil Rebilas, Darrell Gwynn collection)

At Indy, Darrell qualified the car number one, with Garlits qualifying near the back of the pack. But a contest between the two Florida drivers was inevitable. This time, Darrell thought he had an edge.

"When I was getting ready for the first round, I was putting my shoes on and there was a rock in my shoe," Darrell recalls. "My first instinct was to take my shoe off and get rid of the rock, but then I decided to leave it in. I figured I needed to be a mean son-of-a-bitch to beat Garlits, so I figured by the end of the day, my foot would be bleeding and I'd be angry enough to take him on."

Although Garlits was improving by nearly a tenth every round, Darrell believed he had his friend and rival covered. "But sure enough, he got another tenth better in the final and whipped my butt again at Indy," Darrell says. "That was another one we felt we had in our hands that got away."

No one was more disappointed than Darrell—well, maybe Chris Cunningham. In addition to the big-money purse for winning Indy, a motorcycle was thrown in as an extra incentive. "I remember Chris saying 'That's my motorcycle if we win,'" Darrell says. "To this day, I feel like I owe him a motorcycle."

"There was something about us and bad luck when it came to

Among the elite

Gwynn is newest drag racing star

By MICHAEL GUNSTANSON
Star-Telegram Correspondent

The names of drag racing legends come easily to mind: Garlits, Muldowney, Prudhomme, McEwen and Glidden. Pencil in the name of Darrell Gwynn for one of those coveted spots.

Gwynn is involved in one of the most heated rivalries the sport has known. He and "Big Daddy" Don Garlits have virtually redefined the Top Fuel category. And in the process, the two have tested what once was a good friendship.

"We're still friends," Gwynn said. "But we're competitors at the track. We want to do what it takes to win."

Garlits, who was the first to go 270 mph in a dragster, predicted last year he would break the 280 mph barrier sometime in the near future. Some of his thunder was stolen at the Texas Motorplex/Chief Auto Parts Nationals last September when Gwynn made a 5.28-second run at 278 mph.

"I think it (the rivalry) is one of the best things to happen to the sport," Gwynn said. "Most people remember Shirley (Muldowney) and Don's, but I must say this is the most intense rivalry ever. It's neat and I'm lucky to be a part of it."

Exchanges between the two may not be heated, but they are barbed, at least from Garlits' end.

At the March 22 Gatornationals in Gainesville, Fla., Garlits said records

Please see Gwynn on Page 10

Star-Telegram/RON T. EN

Drag racer Darryl Gwynn says he wants to be the first to bre 280 mph at the Texas Motorplex this weekend.

Garlits, especially in a final-round matchup," Cunningham says. "If we caught him in an early round, we'd do OK, but in the finals, he killed us. I remember going against him in the Big Bud Shootout once, and as Garlits was backing up, I noticed that he had a flat rear tire. I thought we had him, but that son-of-a-bitch beat us with a flat tire."

And about the motorcycle? "Yeah, Darrell still owes me one."

A few races later, Darrell and the team showed up at a new all-concrete track in Dallas. The track was green and Darrell was one of the first cars to make a pass.

"Everyone was looking forward to Dallas," Darrell recalls. "We were chomping at the bit to get on that new track." On just its first

run, Darrell's hot rod blistered the track in 5.26 seconds at 278 mph, besting the national record of 5.34 and 272 mph.

Darrell mowed through the field, defeating Shirley Muldowney, LaHaie, and Hank Endres before meeting Garlits again in the final. "And I choked again," Darrell says with a laugh. "It had been ill-handling all day in the wind and the final was at night. I didn't have a lot of experience at night, so I was a little nervous. We had problems firing it up, I did a short burnout, and he left on me. He drilled me on the light."

Years later, according to Darrell, Garlits admitted to a little treachery, taking the blame off Garlits's crew chief, Herb Parks. When Darrell was having problems getting fired, Garlits gave the order to fire up, instead of offering the courtesy of waiting for Darrell to get fired; he felt they needed every advantage against Darrell's new engine combination.

Garlits recalls: "1986 was the year Darrell really started to show people something. But even with his talent and that engine combination, if I had to put my finger on one thing that made Darrell so successful early in his career, it would have to be his father's experience. Jerry always took care of his parts, always ran very conservative setups ... that was his son in the car, so he wasn't going to send it out on some kind of kamikaze run.

"But don't get me wrong, I'm not taking anything away from Darrell's abilities," Garlits is quick to add. "Good drivers have the ability to totally focus on what they are doing. When they get that rush of adrenaline, everything goes into slow motion. The crowd and everything that is going on outside the car is blanked out and you can swear you can see one light on the tree go dim just as the filament in the next light begins to light up. Darrell was one of those drivers."

After closing out the season with three final-round appearances and a win at Pomona over Joe Amato, Darrell and his band of volunteers finished an impressive second in the Winston points race behind Garlits. Interest in Darrell and the Bernstein-Armstrong

engine combination continued to grow, with deep-pocketed car owner Larry Minor stepping up with a serious offer for Darrell to consider.

Late in 1986, Minor offered Darrell $475,000, his truck, his trailer, and the unlimited resources of everyone he had working for him, if Darrell would become a driver under Minor's umbrella. At the time, Minor also had another dragster and the Miller-sponsored Funny Car. So although he may have had some interest in Darrell, who finished the season second in Winston championship points, the real strategy, quite possibly, was to get Minor's engine combination to match up with the Budweiser-sponsored Funny Car of Bernstein.

Darrell called Kenny and promised not to make the jump, asking instead for Kenny to see if he could find any help in return for his loyalty. "Just get me something—that's all I asked," Darrell says.

LEFT: "This is one of my favorite pictures," Darrell says of this award-winning photo. (Frank Dinkler, courtesyDarrell Gwynn collection)
ABOVE RIGHT: Darrell and Tony Mills enjoy the success of the '87 season. (Darrell Gwynn collection)

TOP LEFT: Jerry, Darrell, and Joan after a record-setting run in Dallas in 1987. (Les Welch) **TOP RIGHT:** Both Bernstein and Darrell were winners at the 1988 Seafair Nationals in Seattle, making it a Budweiser sweep. The event coincided with Jerry's birthday, and Darrell gave his dad the perfect present. (Les Welch) **BOTTOM RIGHT:** Another Bud sweep. Darrell and Kenny Bernstein celebrate with Bob Glidden at the '88 Keystone Nationals in Maple Grove, Pennsylvania. (Les Welch) **BOTTOM LEFT:** In victory lane at the 1988 Springnationals. Remembers Darrell: "It was our third national event win in a row. Man, were we smiling." (Auto Imagery)

Bernstein went to work and, after numerous meetings with Budweiser, secured $200,000 for Darrell, teaming the two together as Budweiser's one-two nitro punch for 1987. The beer battle was far from over, however, as Minor set his sights on Armstrong.

An offer was on the table—$1 million for three years.

"That's when the shit hit the fan," Darrell recalls. "The number went public very quickly, and Kenny was being pushed to step up in order to keep Dale and maintain his dominance in the division."

In 1987, the Kid began a maturation process, going through media training with Fleishman-Hillard in St. Louis and joining the ranks of the drag racing elite in his role as corporate spokesperson for Budweiser.

Darrell, however, still preferred a dirty T-shirt and jeans to a suit and tie, so the transformation took time. "I remember Kenny and his girlfriend, Sheryl Johnson, asking me to go to an event and questioning me as to what kind of suits I had," Darrell says. "I didn't

have any suits—not one. So, Sheryl took me to a big mall in Costa Mesa, California, and got me fitted for a suit, shirt, and tie and polished me up a little. It was like putting white walls on a garbage truck."

"There was no such thing as business casual back then," recalls Sheryl, who later married Bernstein. "Most racers were used to just being racers and Darrell was no different. He didn't know his neck size or his coat size, and I think for some time his father tied his ties. Darrell packed them pretied in his suitcase so he could just slip them over his neck and tighten them."

ABOVE: Darrell and Eddie Hill in the final of the 1989 Gatornationals. (Auto Imagery) **RIGHT:** "Ken Veney was the mastermind behind much of our success," Darrell says of his crew chief. "He has an unbelievable ability to create horsepower." (Darrell Gwynn collection)

Darrell enjoyed his time with Kenny and Budweiser, traveling around with Armstrong and having a ball. "You aren't supposed to have that much fun," Darrell says. "We just enjoyed every minute of it. I still owe Dale for some of the things he did for me."

On the track, both teams did well in 1987. Darrell won four national events, including a repeat at the fall race in Pomona, where he defeated Michael Brotherton, Connie Kalitta, Eddie Hill, and Dick LaHaie. And he did so without a crew chief, making a lot of the tuning decisions with guidance from Armstrong and friend Ray Alley.

In 1988, however, the relationship began to show signs of strain as Kenny began to struggle while Darrell was in the middle of his best year ever. Darrell won three consecutive events in the Budweiser dragster—Memphis, Baton Rouge, and Columbus—en route to a career-best six-win season and a second-place finish in championship points to Joe Amato.

"We weren't overshadowing Kenny by any means," Darrell recalls. "He had already won two or three Winston championships, but I think the Funny Car was getting a little old for him. He had survived a bad fire, and I think he was ready to do something different.

"I remember he called me up and said 'Well, this is where it ends. Budweiser is not going to renew a second car, and more than likely, you're going to see me in a dragster next year.' Even though I remember how angry I was at the time, I appreciate now just how much I benefited from our relationship."

Darrell admits to believing for a long time that Bernstein was not comfortable in a teammate relationship. He later realized, however, just how much he had learned from the experience and that it was Bernstein who had helped him along to the next level of drag racing success.

"All in all, it was a great learning experience," Darrell says. "I wish I had it all to do over again, because I was so young when I was with Kenny. I could have learned even more if I was just a year or two more

mature. I just wasn't ready to be like Kenny."

Off the track in 1988, Darrell began to pursue his growing interest in family friend Lisa Hurst, calling her often from the road and trying to convince her to join him at a race.

"I still had a few girlfriends during that time, but I really believed there was something special about Lisa," Darrell says. "I'd be out to dinner after a race, leave my girlfriend at the table with my friends, and I'd find a phone to call Lisa. I still remember her dorm number at the University of Miami."

Says Lisa: "I knew he raced, but I didn't really know anything about racing. When he called, it was never to brag about himself—it was just friendly conversation. I would rattle on about what I was doing in college, and he would talk about what city he was going to or something that happened at the track."

The pair talked on the phone for several months, with Lisa politely declining date offers several times, not quite sure if she was ready to risk the long-standing friendship. But Darrell was persistent.

"He never took things personally when I said no," Lisa recalls.

"He would just say things like 'good things come to those who wait.' That really impressed me." The persistence paid off months later, with Lisa agreeing to a summer lunch meeting at Shooters restaurant on North Miami Beach.

"It was a casual, low-pressure lunch date," Lisa says. "I walked away from the date thinking 'Wow, he's a really nice guy.' Our senses of humor were similar, and we just laughed a lot, especially when I spilled salsa on my white jeans. That was a real plus for me."

The childhood friends continued conversing on the phone over the next few months, with Lisa continuing her premed studies at Miami and Darrell finishing the '88 race season.

Some of the calls, however, were more difficult than others. At a race in Houston, with Darrell sitting on his bed in the hotel room talking to Lisa on the phone, friends Ralph Gorr and Dennis Lamonte were busy trying to negotiate the purchase of a live lobster from the manager of a local restaurant.

A little persistence and $25 later, the pair headed back to the hotel with their two-clawed friend. Entering the room, Lamonte lifted Darrell's sweatshirt and threw the lobster onto his chest. Jumping to his feet and losing the phone, Darrell rushed outside and hurled the confused crustacean into the hotel pool.

Later in the year, while Lisa was competing in the Miss Miami Beauty Pageant, Darrell made another run at spending some time

together—sitting in the pageant audience. "While all the girls were getting ready in the hotel room the day of the pageant, the TV happened to be on NBC and a taped broadcast of Darrell's race was on," Lisa says. "It was the Winston Finals and he had just won the race and I'm telling all the girls

'Oh my God, the guy I'm kinda-sorta dating is on TV.' That was the first time I realized what he did and I was really impressed.

"And again, he never made a big deal about it with me," she adds. "He never bragged about all that was going on his life. Here he is a rising star in drag racing, and I never really knew it until that day."

The first "official date," as Darrell calls it, was a Kenny G concert in November, followed by a movie the next night. "We had a great time, and I figured we'd see each other the next week," Darrell says. "But the next night, I got a call from Joe Amato and he wanted me to join him and some friends at Joe's Stone Crabs."

Hesitant to push for three dates on three consecutive days, Darrell almost didn't make the call, but eventually extended the invitation. Lisa happily accepted.

From that point on, both Darrell and Lisa believed they had found something special in each other, with Lisa moving into Darrell's condo a few months later.

"It wasn't like I was thinking this is the guy I'm going to marry," Lisa recalls. "I didn't think about marriage with anyone I dated, but

things with Darrell clicked right away and we knew we didn't want to be with anyone else. We just felt so comfortable with each other. We enjoyed each other's company and we were into each other. We just didn't want to be apart."

With things falling into place away from the track, Darrell's attention returned to his sponsorless race car—a car that had won six races the year before.

The machine would not sit unpainted for long, however, as Darrell got a call from the Jolly Rancher candy company and flew to Chicago to negotiate a deal. "When I got home, there was a FedEx on my table from Jolly Rancher with a contract inside," Darrell says. "But at the same time there were rumblings that Coors was going to make a bigger investment in the sport."

Coors had already thrown a little money at drivers in the NHRA, including Tom McEwen and Dan Pastorini. But when the beer maker's marketing team decided it was going to put a serious effort behind its drag racing interests, Coors executive Steve Saunders started snooping around the pits, looking for the right driver.

According to Saunders, the demographic was right as the "case a week, change your own oil crowd" was perfect for an up-and-

coming beer company. But they still needed the right spokesperson. "The first time I heard any reference to Darrell Gwynn was when I overheard Pastorini cussing him at the racetrack," Saunders says. "He kept wishing bad luck on the Kid, hoping he'd blow up each round. Until then, Coors didn't know Darrell Gwynn from Adam."

Darrell approached Saunders a few weeks later, and the two began discussing the possibilities. But with the Jolly Rancher paperwork sitting on the table, Darrell needed Coors to put a deal together in a hurry if they wanted to move forward.

The deal was negotiated in less than forty-eight hours.

"I went from having no sponsor to having two sponsors ready to make a deal," Darrell says. "And the money was very similar. I just had the feeling that Coors was going to do more to activate the sponsorship in a big way, which meant more in-store signage, more public appearances and joint activities with their NASCAR driver, Bill Elliott. I felt like they cared about me and they were going to wrap their arms around our program."

Darrell took the Coors deal, leaving an open door for fellow Top Fuel driver Lori Johns to accept the Jolly Rancher opportunity. "Now, I'm driving down the road pinching myself," Darrell recalls. "I have a new sponsor, a new look to the race car, and a new girlfriend that I'm crazy about. I just kept wondering what I had done to deserve all that I was getting that year."

At the season opener in Pomona, with the colors of Coors' new beer, Extra Gold, on the dragster, Darrell qualified fifth, knocking off Eddie Hill in the first round before falling to Frank Bradley in the second round.

Moving on to Gainesville after going out in the first round in Houston, Darrell again qualified the new Coors car fifth. He defeated Michael Brotherton in the first round, Dennis Forcelle in the second, and Earl Whiting in the semis, and he collected his first Gatornationals Top Fuel title with a 5.08 in the final against Hill.

"It was getting late and Gainesville didn't have many lights at that time, but not a single person left," Darrell says. "All my high school buddies were there, and we had one of the biggest winner's circle celebrations ever. You needed a wide-angle lens to get everyone in the shot."

The good news continued in '89 as Darrell asked Lisa to become his wife a few months later. The couple kept it a secret until later in the year, picking out rings together and setting a November 1990 wedding date.

The roller-coaster ride as a racer continued, however, as the car stumbled quite a bit after the Gatornationals, going ten events without making it to a single final. But with Indy just around the corner, the car started to come around.

And Los Angeles County fireman Skip Josenhans was going to make sure of it. Josenhans had helped Darrell for several years when the car raced in Pomona, and the car always seemed to run well in California, so Josenhans was going to bring some of that Pomona magic to Indy.

"When he arrived at Indy, his legs were all scarred up and we were wondering what the heck happened," Darrell says.

At dinner that night, Josenhans told the story. He bought a rabbit's foot with plans to rub it on the right lane of the track at the Pomona fairgrounds, the site of three Gwynn victories in the three years prior. Unable to find an open gate, the L.A. County fireman decided to climb the fence.

Josenhans got his pants leg stuck in the barbed-wire fence, bloodied his leg, and finally made it over, only to be confronted by a guard who had spotted him and threatened to throw him in jail. Josenhans pleaded with the guard, explaining what he was trying to do, and the guard reluctantly let him finish his mission. "I told him 'Skipper, that rabbit's foot is going in my hot rod,'" Darrell says. "So, we put that

LEFT: Darrell stands on the engine as the car comes down the return road at the Keystone Nationals in Maple Grove, Pennsylvania. "Two weeks after winning the U.S. Nationals, we set the national ET record and won the race," Darrell says. "Things were going real well." (Auto Imagery) ABOVE: At the 1990 Gatornationals, Darrell once again defeated Eddie Hill. (Darrell Gwynn collection)

LEFT: Decal from Gatornationals in 1990. **BOTTOM LEFT:** "We do clean up nice, don't we?" remarks Darrell. Here the crew gathers for Chris Cunningham's wedding during the off-season. (Darrell Gwynn collection) **BELOW:** "After winning the Gatornationals and before rushing into the press room, I noticed Grandma waving and I had to go give her a big ol' hug and kiss," remembers Darrell of this photo of himself with his grandmother, Elaine Walker. "This is one of my favorite pictures in the world." (Darrell Gwynn collection) **RIGHT:** Darrell and Lisa celebrate. (Darrell Gwynn collection)

rabbit's foot in the car, and the good stuff just started happening."

Darrell qualified the car number one, knocking off Robert Rheehl, Gary Ormsby, and Eddie Hill to set up a U.S. Nationals final with Dick LaHaie. Not only did Darrell collect the win and set a new national mark of 4.981, but he also became the seventh member of the Cragar four-second club with his effort.

After the race, Darrell was quoted in *National Speed Sport News:* "We won six times last year and only twice this year, but this one feels like all six." From that day on, the rabbit's foot stayed in the car, Darrell rubbing it for luck every time he warmed up the engine.

And the luck continued. Darrell won the next race, the Keystone Nationals at Maple Grove, qualifying number two and beating Frank Cook, Jim Head, LaHaie, and Amato. In the semifinal matchup with LaHaie, Darrell set another national record, blistering the rural Pennsylvania track in 4.951 seconds.

In the season's final four events, Darrell finished runner-up twice (Dallas and Phoenix) and qualified number one at the season finale in Pomona, before red-lighting in the second round to Ormsby, giving Ormsby the season title. Darrell finished the season third in Winston championship points, behind Ormsby and Amato.

As the team prepared for the 1990 season, Darrell again had the confidence he felt in 1983 when the team won the alcohol dragster title. "We had some experience under our belt, and I really believed we knew the things to do and not to do in order to win a Winston championship," Darrell says. "It was time to focus all our energy on the championship."

After getting off to a respectable start, the team rolled into Gainesville to defend its Gatornationals title. And Darrell and the boys didn't disappoint.

Qualifying number one, Darrell took out Richard Holcomb, Don

Prudhomme, and Dick LaHaie, setting up another meeting with Eddie Hill in the final. Just as he had done the year before, Darrell beat Eddie.

"It was even better than the first one," Darrell recalls. "Winning Gainesville was just awesome, and it backed up the feeling that we could contend for the championship. At that point, we were just 100 points out of the points lead."

"I remember standing over on the sidelines, watching Darrell win the race under the lights and looking over at the starting line and seeing Lisa jumping around in tight jeans and a white shirt," says friend and former Funny Car champ Frank Hawley. "I just kept thinking how nice it must be to be Darrell Gwynn. He was fast, she was beautiful, and you could see how bright the future was for the two of them."

After a runner-up performance at the Winston Invitational in Rockingham, North Carolina, Darrell had his sights set on Atlanta. But first, he had to take care of some business in England.

After making the trip across the ocean, Darrell would never race again.

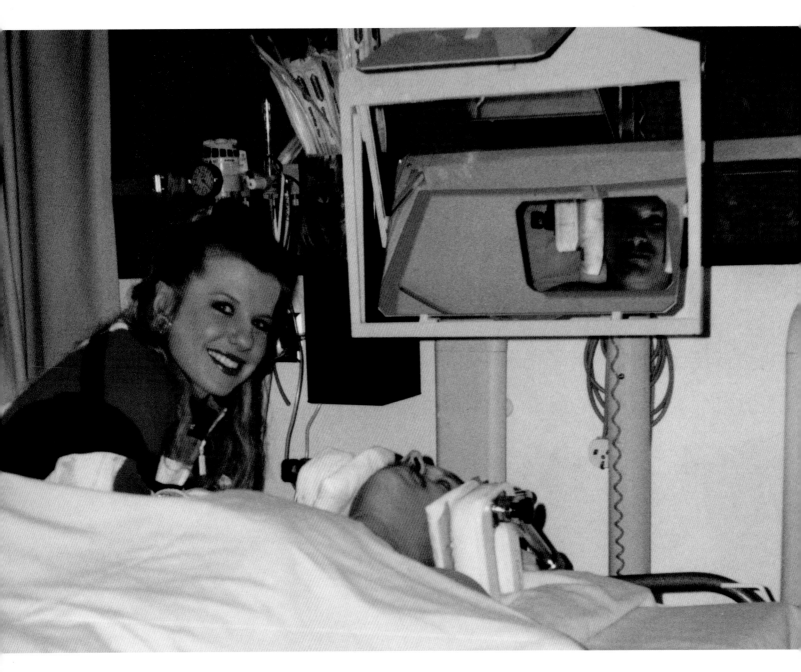

Chapter Six: Thirty-five Days of Hell

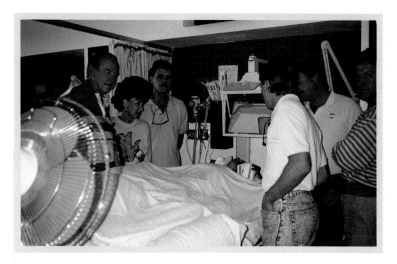

Carl Ruth jumped on a plane to South Florida and drove a rental car to Darrell's condo, where the pair readied for the April trip to Santa Pod.

Lisa didn't want Darrell to go.

"I hated it when he went to England," Lisa says. "I absolutely hated it. I didn't know how safe it was over there, and I knew he didn't have his regular crew with him. The day he left, he kissed me good-bye and closed the door—I cried my eyes out."

Less than two weeks away from taking her medical aptitude tests, Lisa had graduated premed from the University of Miami in 1989 and was working at the Bascom Palmer Eye Institute doing AIDS research. While Darrell was in England, the reigning Orange Bowl Queen got the call she feared more than any other.

Ronnie Hughes broke the news to his niece. Darrell had crashed. His injuries were life threatening. Details were sketchy at first. The first report from Ronnie was that Darrell had broken his back. But all Lisa wanted to know was "Is he conscious? Is he talking?"

Back in England, Darrell was lucky to be alive.

Freed from the remains of his smoldering race car, Darrell had been hurried into an ambulance and driven away from the rural track over a freshly plowed field, which made for a jarring ride.

In the ambulance, Darrell asked Carl: "What does a dead limb feels like?"

"He said everything felt hot," Ruth said. "He knew something was wrong."

The first stop, forty-five minutes later, was Northampton General Hospital, a rural clinic Ruth said reminded him more of a veterinarian's office than a hospital because of its no-frills appearance. The stay lasted only a few hours.

"They really couldn't do much for Darrell at the first hospital except give him blood and send him to another hospital," Ruth recalls. "But, looking back, that stop and that blood probably saved his life."

The next hospital was Stoke Mandeville, located 3 miles southeast of the town of Aylesbury in Buckinghamshire. Built during World War II, the hospital had a long history of treating spinal cord injuries, having established its National Spinal Injuries Center in 1944.

There, Darrell immediately went into traction—a system of wires and pulleys attached to his head at one end and a 10-pound weight on the other—as doctors performed microsurgery in an attempt to save his badly mangled left forearm.

Both bones in the forearm, the radius and the ulna, were shattered in the accident. One was surgically shortened nearly an inch in an attempt to reattach it to the elbow with nonmetal pins. Between the two hospitals, doctors pumped 17 pints of blood into a human body that holds only 12.

Overwhelmed by all that was going on around him, Jerry made the painful call home to Joan, telling her of the accident and their son's condition.

"He didn't really give me all the details," recalls Joan, who was

[93]

LEFT: Lisa made it to England just days after the accident and was comforted by being able to speak with Darrell. Engaged to be married at the end of the 1990 race season, their relationship was put to the ultimate test. (Darrell Gwynn collection) **ABOVE:** Crew members join Darrell and his family in England within days of the accident. (Darrell Gwynn collection)

celebrating a birthday with a friend. "He said it was bad and I needed to get over there."

Joan had to wait a couple of days for an expedited passport, and she made plans to travel with Lisa.

"We both hung on every word of every phone call, but we knew we weren't getting the whole story," Lisa said. "I wanted so badly to talk with Darrell but he was in no condition to spend time on the phone. It was a very lonely, painful time. I just wanted to be with him. I just wanted to hear his voice."

Back in England, surgery to repair the severed artery in his left arm was somewhat successful, and Darrell remained stable through Monday. Joan and Lisa arrived at Stoke Mandeville on Tuesday, two days after the accident. "The halls seemed to go on forever," Lisa recalls. "I finally saw Jerry and ran up and hugged him. It felt like he collapsed in my arms and he was holding on so tight. I was so happy to finally be with them." When Lisa walked around the curtain to see Darrell, the man she was to marry in just a few months looked at her and said quietly, "I'm sorry. I'm so sorry."

Joan followed, struck by a pungent odor being forced through the air by portable oscillating fans and shocked by the condition of her child's charred face.

"I had no idea the smell was coming from Darrell's arm," Joan says. The injured left arm was not healing properly, and as Joan and Lisa arrived, Darrell was being prepared for yet another operation.

In a personal diary she kept while in England, Lisa recalls Darrell's swollen "raccoon" face and his shortness of breath, but also noted that he was alert and conscious as they rolled him away. "The hospital was so different from ones I had visited in the U.S.," Lisa says. "When we first arrived, Darrell was behind a curtain in an open unit. There was no air-conditioning and the windows were wide open." Adds Joan: "The doctors and nurses were wonderful and Darrell was getting excellent care, but the building seemed to be from another time."

After surgery, doctors informed the family there was a strong possibility Darrell would lose his arm and even if they could save it, use of the mangled limb would be severely limited. Darrell's left hand and forearm had sustained massive soft tissue and muscle damage.

Jerry contacted doctors in the United States for help, turning to Dr. Terry Trammel, an orthopedist whose racing patients had included Rick Mears, Kevin Cogan, Derek Daly, and Shirley Muldowney, and Dr. Barth Green of the Miami Project to Cure Paralysis. Both doctors offered to fly to England with some hope of offering assistance.

"I argued with the doctors over there from the first day about saving his arm," Dr. Green recalls. "They were being very conservative, and I knew we were doing a lot of amazing things in the U.S. with revascularization, so I pleaded with them to get him over here, so we could take a look at the arm."

Looking back, Darrell is convinced his doctors did the right thing.

"Even though Dr. Green thinks he might have been able to save my arm, I was in no condition to travel at the time and it was

X rays - int organs

wasting state - suspends

½ in feeling better
⅟₁₆ oz in per day. good

fell - prick in 4 oz
5 fingers - little strength
in right arm - exercising

Spirits good - Lisa
unbelievable - bad
night - fretful dreams

Lower body - no feeling
for 3 weeks at least
up to 3 months

1st meal - turkey

shake shoulders

Sounds terrific

Church service inground
him. 95 yr sign

Everybody sounded good

Parts don't work too good

Believes in miracles

1 to 1½ ft. of mail everyday

Hotel room - house?

Wonderful caring people

becoming a matter of life and death," Darrell says. "If I could have picked a place to get injured, it certainly would have been South Florida, but I think I got excellent care in England and the doctors helped us make the right decisions at the time."

Although Darrell's arm continued to get a great deal of medical attention from the Stoke Mandeville surgeons over the next two days, no spinal cord surgeries took place in England.

"The standard at Stoke Mandeville was traction rather than surgery," Darrell says. "They simply tried to line the head and neck up where they were supposed to be and let everything grow back together. There were shattered pieces of bone floating around in my neck, and the plan was to leave them there and let nature take its course."

Tuesday night, Darrell slept very little, struggling with fever, night-

ABOVE: Drag racing legends Ed "Ace" McCulloch, Don Prudhomme, and Shirley Muldowney manage the fund-raising area in Atlanta. Darrell's pit area was unused, but the space did not go to waste, as thousands of dollars were raised. (Darrell Gwynn collection)

mares, and troubling hallucinations. At one point he thought that his arms were crossed in front of him while his legs were up over the top of his head. "He was turning green," Lisa says. "He was becoming septic and bacteria were invading his blood."

On Wednesday, the repaired artery in the left arm ruptured and emergency surgery was needed to stop the bleeding. The wound was left open and packed in ice, as Darrell's overall health was beginning to deteriorate. The arm injury was becoming life threatening.

Ever the racer, even as the amputation of the ravaged limb was discussed, Darrell talked with Jerry about the possibilities of continuing to drive the Top Fuel dragster with a prosthetic limb. They never even considered that paralysis could be a lifelong condition.

"The first few days, we just wanted him to survive," recalls Jerry, who refers to the time in England as "thirty-five days of hell." "None of us knew anything about spinal cord injuries, so we weren't thinking about anything but keeping him alive and praying for his survival. Nobody was thinking about the race car except Darrell.

"I told him if he wanted to continue, I'd make it happen," Jerry adds. "Or we could quit racing altogether. I left it up to Darrell."

Darrell was rolled into surgery yet again, this time to remove the left forearm below the elbow. "I was conscious through everything—the accident, the ride to the hospital, everything," Darrell says. "But if there was one time I wish I wasn't awake, it would have been when they took my arm. Hearing the big crack when the giant bolt cutters snapped my bone was not a memory I wanted to keep with me."

But the procedure was successful, and Darrell emerged from the operating room already feeling much better than when he had gone in. "When he came out, we were so relieved," Lisa says. "He looked 100 percent better. From that point on, things were much better."

With Darrell clinging to life in England, word of his accident spread quickly through the drag racing community and fundraising efforts, spearheaded by family friend Joyce Schultz, began immediately.

"I thought everything was over," recalls Chris Cunningham, who got the news from his mother. "I didn't know much after the first call other than that he had lost a lot of blood and that he had a neck injury. I started making plans immediately to get over there."

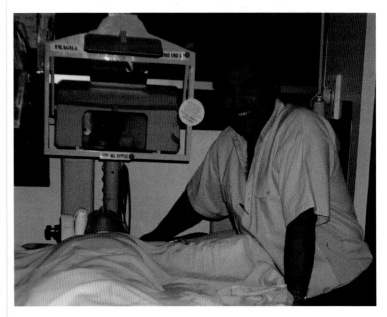

ABOVE: Sheryl Johnson was a key player in raising money for Darrell's recovery fund. Here she shows off funds raised in Atlanta, which was the first race Darrell missed after the accident. (Darrell Gwynn collection)
RIGHT: NHRA chaplain Ken Owen visits Darrell at Stoke Mandeville in England. Darrell's strong faith was a source of strength during a very difficult time. (Darrell Gwynn collection)

"From the first information we were getting, we really thought he was going to die," says Garlits, who first heard of the accident while at his Florida shop. "It was a tough time for all of us just waiting to get more information."

On Friday, Darrell continued to show improvement. In her diary, Lisa wrote that Darrell "began offering money and body parts for a glass of water." His stomach and bowels still weren't working, a common condition after trauma injuries, so he couldn't eat or drink anything for several days.

Away from Darrell only for short periods, Lisa recalls sitting in the hospital cafeteria for the first time, noticing people in wheelchairs and the families that were with them.

"I remember looking around and saying to myself 'Is this going to be us?'" Lisa recalls. "Before that, a wheelchair was a foreign thing, and I certainly never imagined my husband being in one for the rest of his life. But this was still Darrell. He didn't let what happened to him kill his spirit and that is what I loved about him—his spirit. The accident had not changed that one bit."

Over the next few days, Darrell remained stable. A portable pay phone shared by the ward allowed Darrell to make a few phone calls, one of the first to longtime family friend and NHRA announcer Dave McClelland during the Atlanta race weekend.

McClelland recorded several conversations with Darrell, playing them back over the track's public address system and as part of a 900-number NHRA results line.

Darrell's optimism could be heard in his words, but his speech was labored and his breathing difficult.

"I feel good," Darrell says in one of the taped interviews. "Everything is here except my left hand, and I think I can drive without that. We're hoping all my parts will be working in another month or so."

"Darrell and his family were already very close to my family," says McClelland, an NHRA announcer since 1961. "He already had a spe-cial place in our hearts, so when this happened, those feelings were magnified a hundred times—a thousand times—infinitely. Our relationship made the interviews very difficult. But everyone felt it was necessary because so many people wanted to hear from him.

"I don't know a single person comparable to Darrell Gwynn as a human being," McClelland continues. "In my line of work, I have had the opportunity to meet a lot of people—a lot of celebrities in racing and the entertainment industry—but no one comes close to Darrell Gwynn. The way he and his family responded to this tragedy was nothing short of amazing. Darrell is a true miracle."

In Atlanta, Darrell's pit area was left vacant and tables were set up where his car would have been, as the fund-raising efforts continued. News of Darrell's injury spread, and phone calls became more frequent. Joan, however, often relied on others to handle the conversations, saying, "We just couldn't talk about it over and over again. It was too much."

Several days later, Carl Ruth and Chris Hyatt left England, with Carl knowing there was little more they could do to help their injured friend.

"That was a very long plane ride," Ruth recalls. "I remember Chris asking 'Why?' the entire way. He just kept asking the question all the way home."

Back at the hospital, the Gwynns were overwhelmed by the outpouring of support. Wheelchairs overloaded with hundreds of letters and get-well wishes were rolled in every day. More than a hundred flower arrangements were received and filled the room before the family had to start turning them away. "So many people did wonderful things," Joan says. "We felt so lifted—so positive.

"People asked me later if I was ever mad about what happened, but I never was," Joan continues. "I was sad and a part of me died the day I first walked into that hospital room, but we still had Darrell and I knew our family could still make memories."

The first few nights, people slept where they could, on chairs or on mattresses on the floor, to stay close to Darrell. Showers were taken at the hospital. It wasn't until days later that anyone would consider staying in a hotel room.

A few days after the accident, a letter arrived from home. The insurance company that had been covering Darrell for years decided within days of his accident that it didn't want to carry him anymore. According to Jerry, the agency even tried to return the more than $10,000 in premiums the Gwynns had paid over the life of the policy.

"We had just sent them a payment a month before the accident, and they cashed the check," Jerry says. "There was never a single problem, and then a week or so after the crash, we got a letter saying Darrell wasn't covered."

The decision would be argued in court for years, with final settlements nowhere near the costs involved in Darrell's immediate and long-term care.

On Monday, April 23, Darrell's stomach and bowels finally started working again, his bloated waistline dropping 3 centimeters. His breathing improved dramatically.

On Tuesday, Darrell was feeling a little stronger, especially in his right arm. He watched TV while Jerry went with NHRA official and family friend Steve Gibbs, who had arrived earlier in the week, to examine the remains of the race car.

"The car was being kept in a World War II Quonset hut at Santa Pod," Gibbs recalls. "The driver's cage itself was intact. In fact, I think it could have been used again."

The accident had broken the car into three main pieces: the front end and roll cage, the winged rear end, and the motor. Everything was laid out neatly on the floor of the storage area.

"It took Jerry some time to get the energy and to get himself emotionally stable enough to look at the car," Gibbs said. "He was asking a lot of questions of himself, and I knew he was hurting

real bad."

On Wednesday, Darrell was allowed small amounts of water every hour. Lisa wrote in her diary that the "vitamin milkshake" he had been receiving through a vein in his right arm was removed. Most of the day, the family read Darrell a selection of cards from the ever-growing pile and scratched the itches that came with the healing burns on his face.

On Thursday, Darrell ate his first food since the accident—chicken soup—and he reached a few other milestones as well. Darrell was allowed to drink as much as he liked throughout the day. The hospital staff also began weaning him from the oxygen mask,

and Darrell made it through the entire night without it.

But the improvements proved a double-edged sword. Darrell's expectations began to rise as his strength returned. In her diary, Lisa wrote: "He's beginning to get impatient and is 'anxious to walk out of the hospital.' We keep telling him that only time will tell."

Darrell, however, knew his chances of walking again were slim.

"I knew most of it was very likely permanent, simply because of the velocity of my accident," Darrell says. "It's not like I walked into

ABOVE: The entire drag racing community rallied around its fallen star. (Darrell Gwynn collection)

a pole and broke my neck at 2 mph. It was a 240-mph whiplash.

"Doctors explained to me later that a spinal cord has the same consistency as a strawberry, and it certainly doesn't take much to bruise a strawberry," Darrell adds. "I knew my spinal cord was probably a mess. But I still had hope. My spinal cord was not severed, so they referred to it as an 'incomplete' injury. Had it been a 'complete' injury, I would have had no chance in hell to recover."

Thursday also marked the first visit from Darrell's NHRA sponsor. Steve Saunders, who had been called by crewman Nick Floch, arrived with "a hockey bag filled with ten cases of Coors, T-shirts, hats, and anything else that would fit."

"When I got there and saw Darrell, I was in shock," Saunders says. "We held hands and we cried. He kept apologizing and I kept trying to tell him that he didn't owe us anything. This was so much bigger than that."

Just two weeks earlier, Saunders and his family had joined Darrell and Lisa for some vacation time in the Florida Keys prior to the Gainesville race, tooling around together on Jet Skis. "It was heartbreaking in so many ways," Saunders says. "Everything was going so great just a few weeks before. Darrell and Lisa were planning to get married, and we were having a lot of fun together with the race team."

Depression began to set in for Darrell on Friday, as Lisa noticed him staring off into space much of the time—time Darrell says he spent "counting dots and cracks in the ceiling."

More visitors arrived, including three-time Top Fuel champion Shirley Muldowney, offering encouragement and company to their fallen friend. Muldowney, who had been bedridden for seventeen months while recovering from a life-threatening racing accident of her own in 1984, brought checks, letters, and a long get-well card from the other racers. Braving her first transatlantic flight, the self-admitted nervous flyer wanted to see for herself what kind of condition Darrell was in.

"You could tell everyone was scared," Muldowney recalls. "They contained it well, but it wasn't too hard to read the expressions. Darrell was in a lot of trouble and everyone in the room knew that. As soon as I got home, I started spreading the word that they were going to need some serious help."

Lisa was bolstered by the arrival of her mother and Uncle Ronnie's wife, Diane, who gave her the much-needed emotional support she was looking for from familiar faces. The frequent visitors helped keep Darrell's mind occupied. A nose tube used to drain bile from his stomach was removed, and early meals consisted of cereal for breakfast, soup for lunch, and soup, mashed potatoes, and peas for dinner.

"The food there was the worst I've ever had in my life," Darrell says.

Progress continued on Friday as the heart monitor and last IV were removed. Although Darrell took on his first full meal, turkey casserole, his main form of sustenance continued to be liquid. The frozen orange Otter Pops brought over by Muldowney were never far away.

"The family was very strong, but everyone had their moments," says Muldowney, who stayed for several days. "I only saw Joan cry once and it was when we were alone. She was very worried about what would happen to Darrell after she and Jerry were gone. She wondered who would take care of him. This was her only child."

At home in Florida, Darrell's grandmother, Elaine Walker, made

notes on a pad as she talked with the family: "everybody sounds good ... parts don't work too good ... 1 to 1½ feet of mail everyday ... believes in miracles."

The healing process was painfully slow, but Darrell was encouraged by his improving status. "My heart and lungs were in such good shape that they took me off the machines," Darrell says in one of the McClelland interviews. "I don't have any more hoses—no tubes coming out of my nose or mouth. I'm breathing on my own, and there are no more needles in me."

Sunday, two weeks after the accident, brought a false sense of hope as Darrell's left foot moved. Lisa wrote about the day in her diary: "Early this morning, he moved his left foot as he was reading the get-well card from the races .... We were all elated and, for a moment, we were on top of the world. However, Dr. Hans Frankel visited with us and said it was just a reflex because he couldn't feel his foot moving. The only encouraging thing is that the doctor said the reflex comes first and is an indication that his health is improving. When Darrell can feel his foot moving, that's when we can jump up and down. And so far, there has been no change in his level of feeling."

Sunday also marked the first day of serious discussion about the fate of the race team, with Darrell wanting to continue the program with a different driver.

Jerry, however, was ready to call it quits.

"I could have walked away and never looked back at that point," Jerry says. "But Darrell wanted to keep going, and if Darrell was going to do it, I was going to give him all the support I could manage."

Chris Cunningham also noticed a change in Jerry. "I didn't think I'd ever see them at a racetrack again after seeing Jerry in England," Cunningham said. "I don't know if he felt guilty or just hurt, but Darrell's accident took a lot out of him. He wasn't the same."

Darrell, however, wasn't ready to give up, calling family friend and former Funny Car champion Frank Hawley. "He said he was

LEFT: Pete Brozene, a friend Darrell met through Carl Ruth, painted his alcohol Funny Car with a special Darrell Gwynn Get Well Soon paint scheme. (Darrell Gwynn collection) **ABOVE:** Chassis builder Mark Rowe donated this chassis as a fundraising source for Darrell's recovery fund. The raffle sold thousands of tickets. (Darrell Gwynn collection)

BELOW: NHRA Funny Car driver John Force, who would go on to win twelve national championships and become the sport's winningest driver, carries a "Get Well Soon Darrell" sticker inside his car. (Darrell Gwynn collection) RIGHT: A newspaper article announces Frank Hawley as Darrell's chosen driver.

calling me because he knew I could drive the car and because he trusted me not to take his sponsor," Hawley says. "All I could do was picture him there lying in the bed motionless with Jerry holding the phone to his ear. I already knew what my answer was, but Darrell wanted me to be sure, so he suggested we wait a day and think about it to make sure I wasn't reacting on emotion.

"Before I got the call, word had already spread that they wanted to keep the team going and every driver I knew would have said yes to driving that car," Hawley adds. "It was one of the fastest cars in the country, and race car drivers like to drive fast cars. But there was no excitement about it, because we all knew why the ride was available."

The next day, Hawley called back and said yes.

From Lisa's diary: "We were all very proud of Darrell for the way he handled the situation, because we know how hard it was for him to put someone else in his car. However, I know he is relieved a decision has been made and he can concentrate on his recovery .... He wasn't in too good of spirits today. Reality is really setting in."

As the days wore on, Darrell's battered body continued to recover, with more reflex episodes, but still no feeling. His body was tested daily with blunt and sharp "prick tests" to measure any changes in his level of feeling. Battles with early-morning depression were more frequent. His left arm was still in the healing process. Dead tissue and discharge were removed regularly as nurses changed the dressing three times a day.

From Lisa's diary: "Our days have gone by quicker because of all the mail to read. It has been a blessing to hear from people who have gone through what we have and made it. We just have to keep pumping that into Darrell—there's always hope. And we have to continue to believe that this all happened for a reason. Only the Lord knows, but hopefully someday we will understand."

On Wednesday, May 2, the family began talking with doctors about moving Darrell back home to a hospital in Miami, a journey that was still weeks away.

Thursday brought a move to a different hospital ward, up the stairs from St. Francis to St. George. Darrell had recovered enough to make the move, and St. Francis was overcrowded. But the move proved to be an ordeal, and his new room had six beds, leading to a lot more noise and activity. Darrell seemed to get less personal attention.

Lisa would stay with Darrell for "the night shift," and in the morning, she would grab a few hours of sleep on a cot in a vacant hospital room when everyone else returned from the hotel.

Thursday night, a television arrived along with a video of Darrell's crash. "It's a miracle he's still alive," Lisa wrote in her journal after viewing the tape. To cheer everyone up, the family watched a "Get Well Darrell" tape put together by Diamond P Productions, in part during the race weekend in Atlanta, with Steve Evans interviewing nearly everyone at the track.

[102]

Hawley will take over Darrell Gwynn's car

By SCOTT FOWLER
Herald Sports Writer

Frank Hawley was given the chance to drive one of the dominant cars in drag racing Thursday, but he wasn't smiling.

"I don't feel like celebrating at all," said Hawley, who will replace Darrell Gwynn for the rest of the season in the Coors Extra Gold Top Fuel Dragster. "If I didn't know Darrell's family as well, maybe I would. I know there are tens of thousands of people who'd like to drive this car, and under different circumstances it would be a great opportunity . . . now, I've got mixed feelings about it."

Darrell Gwynn, a North Miami native, was paralyzed from the chest down in a racing accident in Bedfordshire, England, April 15. He was scheduled for a 6- to 8-hour spinal surgery today, but that has been postponed until early next week because of other health problems. Gwynn has a urinary infection and also has been running a fever as high as 104 degrees, a spokesman for The Miami Project to Cure Paralysis said.

"The doctors just want to be careful and make sure everything is cleared up before surgery," said Susan Fitzpatrick, the Project's director of education. "It may be Monday or Tuesday now." The operation is designed to give Gwynn some controlled movement of his right hand — his chance of walking again is only three to five percent.

Against that sober backdrop, Hawley and Darrell's father Jerry Gwynn went ahead with a press conference Thursday announcing Hawley's appointment. Gwynn, who was team manager for his son, will continue in that role for Hawley and will travel to each of the races in which the team participates. The first will be the Springnationals in Kirkersville, Ohio, June 7-10. Jerry Gwynn made a commitment to Hawley only through the end of this season.

"It'll probably be pretty difficult, running without Darrell," the elder Gwynn said. "But Darrell wanted to do this. He wanted to take care of the people who took good care of him during the lean years."

Hawley, 33, is a two-time National Hot Rod Association Funny Car champion and also has experience in the Top Fuel category. He is from Gainesville, where he runs a successful drag racing school.

Breakers to play seven home matches

The Miami Beach Breakers announced a seven-match home schedule that will begin July 11 against the Charlotte Heat in Abel Holtz Stadium at Flamingo Park.

The Breakers, one of nine teams in the Domino's Pizza TeamTennis League, will have four home and five road matches televised on the Sunshine Network. Sandy Collins, Cammy MacGregor, Richard Schmidt and Greg Van Emburgh are on Coach Virginia Brown's squad.

Season tickets vary from $2,500 for a sky box of six seats to $50 for one general admission seat. Individual tickets are $10 general admission, $15 inner circle and $20 box seats, with children under 12 at half price.

For ticket information, call 1-800-749-9557 between 9 a.m. and 4 p.m. Tickets also will be available at Ticketmaster outlets after June 11.

July: 11, Charlotte, 7 p.m.; 14, at Newport Beach; 17, at Los Angeles; 19, at San Antonio; 20, at Raleigh; 22, Los Angeles, 5 p.m.; 24, Sacramento, 7 p.m.; 26, at New Jersey; 27, at Charlotte; 28, San Antonio, 7 p.m.
August: 1, New Jersey, 7 p.m.; 3, Raleigh, 7 p.m.; 4, at Wellington; 5, Wellington, 5 p.m.

As doctors continued to make arrangements to help Darrell travel home, days went by and Darrell continued to receive visitors.

"It was real hard to see him in that condition," Cunningham says. "It seemed like I had just been with him at the racetrack, and all I could think of was this was my best friend, the guy I wrestled with in the front yard when we were kids. How could this have happened?"

While crew members Chris, Gary Clark, and Joe Shaffer were visiting and Darrell was munching on a cheeseburger with extra pickles, the family popped in the NHRA get-well tape that ended with heartfelt words from NHRA photographer Leslie Lovett.

While everyone was laughing, Darrell began to cry. From Lisa's diary: "That caused all of us to start crying and we continued to cry together. It was good for Darrell to finally let out that emotion ... and with the guys being there, it touched Darrell even more."

The next few days were filled with visitors and phone calls. NHRA president Dallas Gardner checked in via phone, as did racing legend A. J. Foyt. The Blue Angels sent a personalized get-well video, flying ace Chuck Yeager checked in, and more calls came from Don Prudhomme, Kenny Bernstein, and Dale Armstrong.

From Lisa's diary: "Thank God for the phone—it has been good therapy."

Lynn Prudhomme, Don's wife, and Sheryl Johnson arrived with American food, goodies, fresh clothes, and updates on fund-raising efforts back home.

"It was a devastating experience," Lynn said. "I was prepared to see Darrell, but I wasn't prepared to see an entire hospital full of patients with spinal cord injuries. The numbers and the stories were overwhelming.

"What made it tougher was feeling so helpless in that environment," Lynn continues. "We were in a foreign country, dealing with socialized medicine. Doctors weren't used to having to explain things or answer questions. It was nearly impossible to get any response from anyone."

As more of the focus switched toward getting Darrell home and finding the plane that could do the job, offers to provide an aircraft came in from Connie Kalitta, Larry Minor, Peter Coors, and U.S. Tobacco. Unfortunately, Darrell needed a commercial flight on a jet that could make the transatlantic flight to Miami without stopping. A medical lifeline flight crew and a supply of oxygen also were necessities.

Sheryl Johnson took on the challenge of arranging the complicated flight.

"We didn't go over there with the intent of doing anything more than offering our support," Sheryl says. "Once we were there, however, we got the sense that Jerry and Joan were so worn down and frazzled. They were just going day to day. We knew we had to get them home, so we started asking the doctors questions like 'Can he be moved?' or 'Is it critical not to move him?' Once we understood that it was safe to move him, we started making the phone calls to set it up."

With Johnson coordinating conference calls between the doctors at Stoke Mandeville and doctors at the Miami Project, Kenny Bernstein was making calls back in the United Staes to sponsors and fellow racers to help fund the flight.

"We just wanted to make sure that our eagerness to get everyone

On Saturday, Darrell listened to church services sent by Racers for Christ and another from a church located two doors down from Darrell's childhood home. He spent a lot of the day listening to music cassettes sent over by family friend Bill Wynne, and in later days spent significant time with NHRA chaplain Ken Owen.

"It's a little weird, but I can't listen to any of that music now," Darrell says. "They sent it over because it was my favorite, but now Kenny G reminds me of being in the hospital in England. It ruined that music for me."

Darrell continued to battle bouts of depression, feeling "discouraged and helpless because he has no control and can't do anything for himself," Lisa wrote.

On Tuesday, May 15, less than a week before the planned return to Miami, Darrell talked about life in a wheelchair for the first time. He wanted to know everything.

From Lisa's diary: "He wanted to know about all the availabilities for people in wheelchairs—cars, sex, etc. I was happy to see him talking about it. He wanted to know why someone didn't come talk about it—I said it's too soon. We aren't sure if he'll even need a wheelchair at this point."

"Reality started to set in as I was having conversations with other patients in the hospital," Darrell says. "I would ask how long they'd been injured and how they were hurt, and I'd get answers like 'I wrecked my car going 30 miles an hour and I've been in a chair for fourteen years.' It started to get pretty obvious that I was going to be in a wheelchair for a long time.

"That's when I started asking questions. I wasn't prepared to deal with life in a wheelchair at all. Nobody is. I needed answers to big questions. How will I make a living? How will I have children? And I needed answers to small questions too. How will I go to the bathroom?"

By Wednesday, May 16, final preparations were being made for Darrell's return to Miami. A halo traction brace being fitted to

home had absolutely no chance of hurting Darrell or causing more injury," Sheryl says. "We were all praying for the miracle that Darrell would walk out of that hospital in England, but when it became obvious it wasn't going to happen, we just wanted to get him home."

By the end of the day on Thursday, May 10, plans appeared set. A May 20 return date was scheduled with British Airways. Despite several days of increased pain in his back and shoulders, as well as occasional hot flashes, Darrell finally had something he could focus on. He was going home.

LEFT: Stickers supporting Darrell's recovery and return were part of the fund-raising effort. **ABOVE:** Fans sign a giant get-well card for Darrell at Le Grandnationals in Montreal, Canada. (Darrell Gwynn collection)

immobilize Darrell's spine was too small, so the procedure would have to wait until Thursday. A doctor came by to visit Darrell with a picture of his bed setup on the plane, and visitors from the ward filed in and out all day to say goodbye.

Lisa noted in her journal that Darrell was being "real sarcastic and obnoxious—his usual self."

On Thursday, Darrell went back to the St. Francis ward for an hour-and-a-half procedure to have the carbon-fiber halo attached to his skull with half a dozen metal screws. The halo was then connected to a well-fitted plastic jacket with a system of rods, virtually immobilizing Darrell's spine—a necessity for travel.

"That was one of the most painful things I had to deal with," Darrell says. "I screamed and yelled as they were shooting needles in my head preparing me for the drill. It hurt so bad. God, I just wanted to get that thing off."

"It was horrible," Lisa says. "When he came out of the procedure room, it was shocking to see screws in his head attached to this big contraption. There was blood on his face and bruises from where they drilled. I was horrified and he was in so much pain.

"But they had to do it to get him home," Lisa adds. "They had to

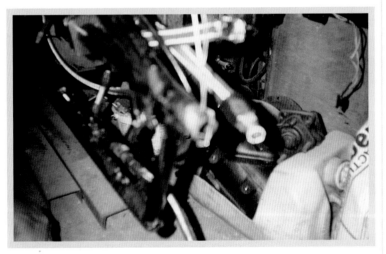

stabilize him for the flight home."

On Saturday, the day before he left, Darrell and his family discovered yet another condition related to his spinal cord injury. When he was rolled over early in the morning, the nurses covered Darrell with only one blanket. By the time Jerry arrived, Darrell's temperature had fallen to 96 degrees Fahrenheit. The disruption to Darrell's nervous system had stopped his body from being able to shiver. Blood vessels controlling skin temperature simply couldn't react.

The staff immediately covered him with more blankets and fed him warm tea, but it wasn't until a few hours later that Darrell's body temperature returned to normal.

The last few hours Darrell spent at Stoke Mandeville were not his most comfortable, and Lisa admits that the fear of an unknown future was taking an emotional toll on everyone.

A day after receiving another special call from Chuck Yeager, Darrell received a visit from a legendary figure in British racing, Formula One team owner Frank Williams. Williams had been paralyzed just a few years earlier in a road accident near the Paul Ricard racing circuit in the south of France, and he made his way through the hospital in his wheelchair to see Darrell.

"There was so much commotion among the staff," Darrell recalls. "It was like the king of England was coming for a visit. There were eighteen-year-old nurses running around saying, 'I can't believe Frank Williams is here.' For someone like that to take time out of his day to visit me meant a lot. I'll never forget it."

Sunday, May 20, five weeks after the crash, Darrell and his family were ready to go home. The lifeline crew arrived at 8 A.M., and the doctor set up the monitoring equipment as Darrell was medicated and moved to an air mattress aboard British Airways flight 293, a commercial flight loaded with passengers. Darrell and his support team occupied eight rows. Within hours, Darrell was on his way to Miami's Jackson Memorial Hospital and the Miami Project to Cure Paralysis.

Says Lisa, "Even though it had been only five weeks, it seemed like forever."

In an ironic twist of fate, just two months before Darrell crashed his Coors Extra Gold dragster during the exhibition run in England, the South Florida native had personally applied a Miami Project to Cure Paralysis sticker to the side of his race car. Darrell and Coors executives had selected the Miami Project as their charity to set up an incentive program that would contribute funds based on Darrell's performance at the racetrack.

The Miami Project, a program founded in 1985 and based at the University of Miami School of Medicine, is the world's largest and most comprehensive research center dedicated to finding more effective treatments and, ultimately, a cure for paralysis that results from spinal cord injury.

"Coors had a big tradition of getting involved with the charity of the driver's choice," Darrell says. "So, when they approached me about a charity, we did some research and came up with the Miami Project. We put some decals on the car and had already donated money based on my win in Gainesville.

"But at the time, I really didn't know much about spinal cord injuries, what a spinal cord does and all that it affects on the human body," Darrell adds. "I remember being at the press conference and talking to people in wheelchairs, never really knowing what they go through on a daily basis. Unless you have someone in your family that has a spinal cord injury, you don't know, and you're not expected to know, all they go through.

"I never knew that one day I would be depending on the same organization I was trying to help."

LEFT: The spot of the break in Darrell's Top Fuel dragster. Jerry and the NHRA's Steve Gibbs examined the car days later at a Santa Pod storage facility. (Darrell Gwynn collection) **ABOVE:** Darrell, his family, and a medical crew took several rows of a commercial jet for the ride home to Florida. The remainder of the plane was filled with regular transatlantic passengers. (Darrell Gwynn collection)

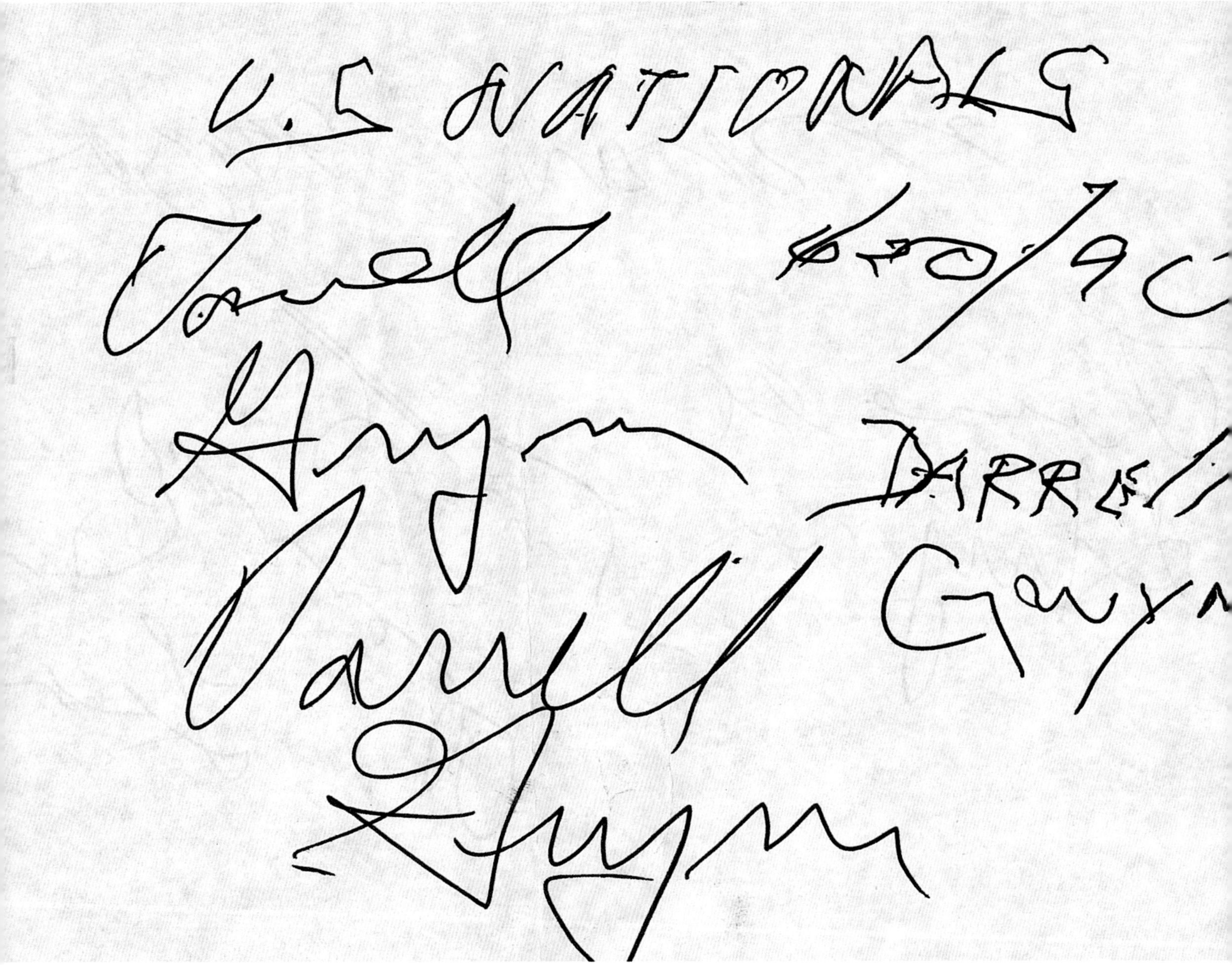

U. S NATIONALS

Tuml

Darrell
Gwyn

DARREL
Gwyn

Daryll
Gwyn

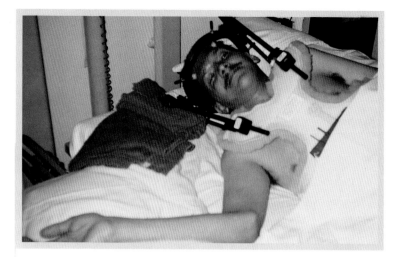

Chapter Seven:
Finding a New Normal

Family friend Bill Lusby sat silently next to Darrell for the ten-minute ambulance trip up Interstate 95 from Miami International Airport to Jackson Memorial Hospital, a teaching facility on the campus of the University of Miami. Lusby had watched Darrell grow up, even taking him to local stock car races as a child. But to Darrell's recollection, no words were exchanged between the two as they rode together to the hospital that day.

"We talked several times on the phone while he was recovering in England, and he kept asking if I was going to be there," says Lusby, who worked for the ambulance company at the time. "The ambulance staff and a couple of people from the airplane also were in there with us, so it was very crowded. I wanted to be there for Darrell. I really didn't need to say anything as long as he knew I was there."

Lowered out of the ambulance at Jackson on May 20, Darrell was bombarded instantly by a cacophony of familiar voices. Unable to turn his haloed head, he recognized friends and family by their greetings. Trying to wave, he struggled to lift his arm.

"I could hear people yelling 'We love you Darrell' or 'Hang in there,'" Darrell says. "I could hear individual voices and pick each one out. It was a very cool feeling—very comforting."

Rolled into room 0725 on the seventh floor of Jackson's west wing, Darrell and his family immediately began meeting with doctors. Dr. Barth Green, then director of the Spinal Cord Injury Unit and president and founder of the Miami Project to Cure Paralysis, took the lead.

A few days after Darrell's arrival, Dr. Green conducted a press conference, telling the world there was less than a 5 percent chance of ever seeing Darrell walk again.

"The velocity of injury is the most important indicator in making a prognosis, and Darrell had the ultimate high-velocity injury," Dr. Green says. "From the first time I evaluated him, I believed Darrell's only hope of walking again would be through the Miami Project with transplantation and regeneration."

Jerry and Joan, both attending the press conference, struggled when they heard the words they already knew were true. Jerry broke down mid-sentence, unable to continue answering a reporter's question. Joan moved closer to comfort her husband.

"I'm supposed to be the 6-foot-3, 250-pound bad ass, but she's the one who kept everyone's spirits up," Jerry says. "She was my strength."

Darrell's first night at Jackson was his worst in weeks as pain from the halo became unbearable. "He screamed and cried in pain like I've never heard him scream," Lisa says of that night. "Doctors finally adjusted the halo and increased his pain medication, but the goal from that moment on was to get him out of the halo and into surgery."

"I think those first days at Jackson were some of the most

LEFT: This is Darrell's first attempt at writing after the accident. "The therapists were wonderful," Darrell says. "They realized how important it was for me to be able to sign my name, and they worked hard to help me get better at it." While at Jackson, Darrell set a goal of being back at the track by the U.S Nationals in September. **ABOVE:** At Jackson Memorial Hospital in Miami, his head in a halo brace, Darrell manages a characteristic smile, despite his painful condition. (Darrell Gwynn collection)

difficult," Darrell says. "There were a lot of new doctors. I wasn't sure about the surgery. My head felt like it was on fire. And all of this was happening within eight miles from my home. To be so close to home and not able to get there was very difficult."

As doctors continued to examine Darrell in preparation for surgery, Jerry followed his son's wishes and went on with the business of the team. He called a press conference to announce that Frank Hawley was taking over the driving duties of the Coors Extra Gold dragster for the remainder of the season. Hawley's first race would be the Springnationals outside of Columbus, Ohio, the first week in June.

"It was a weird situation," Hawley recalls. "There was more attention from the media than anything I had seen in motor sports."

According to Darrell, the decision to keep racing was simple.

"If we were a sponsorless race team and running like crap, it might have been an easy decision the other way," Darrell says. "But the only thing rock bottom about everything we were talking about was that I was injured. Our race team was in good shape and we had very good equipment. I wasn't going to let one bad day in England ruin everything."

With the team officially turned over to Jerry and Frank, Darrell began concentrating on his recovery.

Assigned to the Gwynns nearly upon the family's arrival at Jackson was clinical psychologist Dr. Judy Lasher. She remembers Darrell as a special case from the very beginning. "There are common threads among patients and families dealing with life-altering spinal cord injuries," Dr. Lasher says. "It's common for patients to begin ruminating about all they can't do—the losses, the relationships. They move in and out of depression. In some cases, they just give up.

"Occasionally, however, there is someone very different," Dr. Lasher adds. "Darrell was one of those cases. He wasn't in denial. He was clearly aware of his situation and he never played the victim. Darrell was focused on moving forward in a positive way. It was clear early on that Darrell was determined to keep control of his life. He needed very little from me other than the positive reinforcement of things he and his family were already doing."

The first step in moving forward would be yet another surgery, this time an attempt to repair his spinal canal and to remove the shattered pieces of bone left floating around his spinal cord. A normal canal is tubular. Darrell's was pinched in the shape of an hourglass. The plan was to open the tube in hopes that the relief of pressure on the spinal cord might allow Darrell to regain a little more controlled movement in his right wrist.

"Immediately, I had every X ray, MRI, or scan you could think of to prepare me for decompression surgery," Darrell says. "The way it was explained to me at the time was that there was absolutely no hope of my spinal cord getting any better while the bone fragments were pushing against the cord. There was, however, some hope—whether it was a lot or a little—that if the pressure was removed, I might eventually get some function back.

"When it's put to you like that, it's a no-brainer," Darrell says. "That subtle improvement would make it possible for me to operate

ABOVE: Friends posted a message for Darrell over Interstate 95 at the exit to the Gwynn's home in South Florida. (Darrell Gwynn collection)
RIGHT: A newspaper clipping shows Darrell being delivered to Jackson Memorial Hospital in Miami as Jerry looks on.

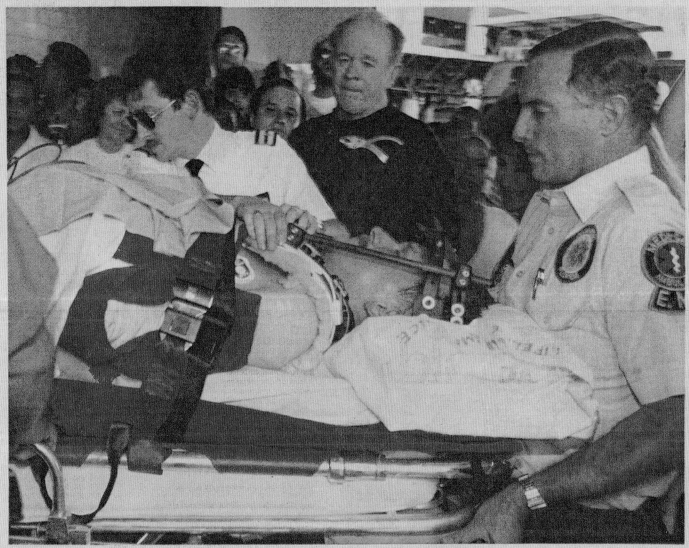

BACK HOME: Darrell Gwynn is wheeled into Jackson Memorial Hospital as his father Jerry Gwynn wears a 'welcome home' ribbon.

Gwynn 'laughs a little bit, cries a lot'

By S.L. PRICE

Herald Sports Writer

Friends, family surround racer

Up on the seventh floor of the west wing at Jackson Memorial Hospital, Room 0725, the television set is on with the sound turned low. A woman on the screen is silently mouthing her love for the telephone company. A sign in the corner of the room is telling the man in the bed, "Welcome Home." But the man in the bed can't see any of it.

Darrell Gwynn is lying on the bed, his head encased in a black steel halo that resembles a bird cage with only four bars. Until it is removed seven weeks from now, the whole of his physical world will be contained within the arc of his eyes. For at least

these few minutes, though, it doesn't matter much. Half a dozen friends are chattering at him from around the bed. More than that wait outside.

On April 15, Gwynn's 1989 Top Fuel dragster smashed into a retaining wall and exploded into flames during a test run in Bedfordshire, England. Gwynn was taken to a hospital in Aylesbury, where doctors removed his left arm below the elbow and told him he was paralyzed from the mid-chest down. Five weeks later, on Sunday, the North Miami native came home.

"How do you like this contraption?" he asks Gary Clark, his chief mechanic, about the stabilizing halo that required four screws in his skull. "You should've seen it. They kept torquing it down, torquing it down." Gwynn laughs. His friends, his mother Joan, his fiancee Lisa Hurst — all laugh.

He is asked how it is, being home. "Obviously, it's a whole different feeling," he says. "When I was there in England, I kept thinking, 'I wish I was home, I wish I was home, I wish I was home.' Now that I'm here, my condition is the same, but my feelings are

different."

Gwynn still has no feeling in the five fingers of his right hand. But as he speaks, his right arm moves back and forth under the sheet and the bed rattles. Gwynn's blond hair is swept off his forehead, and the skin there is tinged yellow and red. There is just a sprinkling of whiskers on his chin, less than you would figure for a 28-year-old. His eyes are very, very blue.

Five weeks have passed since the accident. Mornings, he says, still are the worst for him. Sometimes, when he wakes up, he can almost convince himself this is just a bad

PLEASE SEE **GWYNN, 5D**

'IT'S BEEN DEVASTATING'

DONALD LEVAN / Miami Herald Staff

Jerry Gwynn, father of paralyzed drag racer Darrell Gwynn, is comforted by his wife Joan at a news conference Tuesday at the Jackson Memorial Hospital complex. Dr. Barth Green, right, said Darrell Gwynn has only a '3- to 5-percent' chance of walking again. Darrell is scheduled to undergo a six- to eight-hour operation on his spine Friday. **Story, Page 5C.**

ABOVE: Newspaper clipping of the press conference with Dr. Barth Green telling the world that Darrell's chances of walking again were extremely slim at best.

"Whether someone with Darrell's injuries even survives or not has a lot to do with the family," Dr. Green says. "We can have two patients with the same injury and one can die and one can live because of family support."

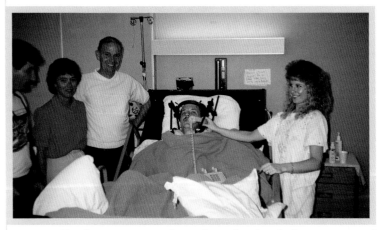

an electric wheelchair, hold a small cup, and lift light objects. I remember rolling into surgery hoping and praying that the operation was going to help."

The procedure itself was postponed several days while Darrell battled heterotopic ossification, the abnormal development of bone, in his hip and a fever of 104 degrees Fahrenheit. Over more than eight hours on June 4, a team of doctors, led by Dr. Green, removed the front half of the fractured fifth vertebra to relieve pressure on the spinal cord. A piece of bone from Darrell's hip was used to fuse the bones above and below the removed vertebra. Once complete in the front, Darrell was turned over on a rotating bed and the process was repeated with the rear half of the damaged vertebra. With the new bone in place, wire was wrapped around the joints at the back of the neck, providing support until the area healed.

After surgery, Darrell was rolled to the intensive care unit in a rotating bed used to shift fluids around and prevent clotting. Staying in the same position for too long could result in a pulmonary embolism and sudden death. Physical therapists, led by senior therapist David Messina, began working with Darrell almost immediately, moving and stretching his arms, shoulders, and lifeless legs for nearly thirty minutes each day.

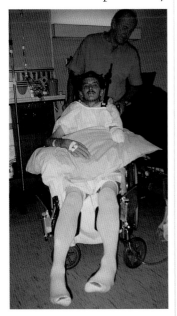

Once out of the intensive care unit, the therapy became more rigorous.

Says Messina: "That's when the hard stuff began. Darrell had to be reintroduced to gravity. From the time of the injury, his entire body had been supported. It was a learning process just to be able to sit in a wheelchair."

Darrell's chest was encased in a sheepskin-lined plastic vest to aid in upper-body stability. Over the next few weeks, he was placed in a reclining chair, raised one notch at a time until he was comfortable in a sitting position.

Along with the physical therapy came occupational therapy and a lengthy training process for family members and friends, as they slowly absorbed all that was involved in caring for someone with a serious spinal cord injury. Jerry, Joan, and Lisa were among those attending seminars on catheterization, bowel programs, transferring techniques needed to lift and move Darrell, and product demonstrations.

"Whether someone with Darrell's injuries even survives or not has a lot to do with the family," Dr. Green says. "We can have two patients with the same injury and one can die and one can live because of family support. The doctors and nurses can give the same treatment, but the patient needs courage and a reason to live and that's where support can make all the difference."

The programs were conducted on a weekly basis in a classroom setting. As many as twenty other spinal cord patients and their families were coming to terms with their injuries at the Miami Project rehab center during the same time.

ABOVE: Still in the halo, Darrell's arm is healing and Jerry helps transport him back to his bed. "Just learning to sit in a chair was part of the recovery process," Darrell recalls. (Darrell Gwynn collection) **ABOVE RIGHT:** Talking with well-wishers on the phone continued to be a source of comfort for Darrell as calls came in from everywhere. Here, Lisa helps with the phone as Darrell's crew chief, Ken Veney, and his wife, Rona, join Tony Mills, left, at Darrell's bedside. (Darrell Gwynn collection)

[113]

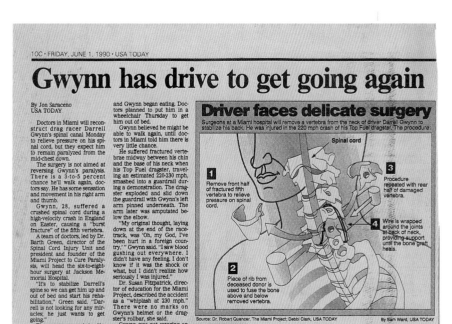

10C • FRIDAY, JUNE 1, 1990 • USA TODAY

Gwynn has drive to get going again

By Jon Saraceno
USA TODAY

Doctors in Miami will reconstruct drag racer Darrell Gwynn's spinal canal Monday to relieve pressure on his spinal cord, but they expect him to remain paralyzed from the mid-chest down.

The surgery is not aimed at reversing Gwynn's paralysis. There is a 3-to-5 percent chance he'll walk again, doctors say. He has some sensation and movement in his right arm and thumb.

Gwynn, 28, suffered a crushed spinal cord during a high-velocity crash in England on Easter, causing a "burst fracture" of the fifth vertebra.

A team of doctors, led by Dr. Barth Green, director of the Spinal Cord Injury Unit and president and founder of the Miami Project to Cure Paralysis, will head the six-to-eight-hour surgery at Jackson Memorial Hospital.

"It's to stabilize Darrell's spine so we can get him up and out of bed and start his rehabilitation," Green said. "Darrell is not looking for any miracles; he just wants to get going."

The surgery, originally scheduled May 25, was postponed because of a urinary tract infection and fever Gwynn developed since his May 20 return from England. The fever broke Wednesday,

and Gwynn began eating. Doctors planned to put him in a wheelchair Thursday to get him out of bed.

Gwynn believed he might be able to walk again, until doctors in Miami told him there is very little chance.

He suffered fractured vertebrae midway between his chin and the base of his neck when his Top Fuel dragster, traveling an estimated 220-230 mph, smashed into a guardrail during a demonstration. The dragster exploded and slid down the guardrail with Gwynn's left arm pinned underneath. The arm later was amputated below the elbow.

"My original thought, laying down at the end of the race track, was 'Oh, my God, I've been hurt in a foreign country,'" Gwynn said. "I saw blood gushing out everywhere. I didn't have any feeling. I don't know if it was the shock or what, but I didn't realize how seriously I was injured."

Dr. Susan Fitzpatrick, director of education for the Miami Project, described the accident as a "whiplash at 230 mph." There were no marks on Gwynn's helmet or the dragster's rollbar, she said.

Gwynn was not wearing an arm restraint. He planned to make only half a pass down the dragstrip at Santa Pod Raceway in Bedford, England. His dragster, which had won a record seven national races dur-

ing a 12-month period ending in 1989, recently had been sold.

Jerry Gwynn, the racer's father, said his son was "always very safety-conscious."

"He was just destined (to crash) on that day, on that race track," Jerry Gwynn said. "The hardest thing now is accepting that he probably won't walk

again, and his desire to race. He'll be a big part of racing, no matter what. Driving is out of the question, at least for a while. Hope never goes away."

Driver faces delicate surgery

Surgeons at a Miami hospital will remove a vertebra from the neck of driver Darrell Gwynn to stabilize his back. He was injured in the 220 mph crash of his Top Fuel dragster. The procedure:

Spinal cord

1 Remove front half of fractured fifth vertebra to relieve pressure on spinal cord.

2 Piece of rib from deceased donor is used to fuse the bone above and below removed vertebra.

3 Procedure repeated with rear half of damaged vertebra.

4 Wire is wrapped around the joints at back of neck, providing support until the bone graft heals.

Source: Dr. Robert Quencer, The Miami Project; Debbi Clark, USA TODAY   By Sam Ward, USA TODAY

The numbers are stunning: there are ten thousand spinal cord injuries a year in the United States, with motor vehicle accidents the number one cause. According to Dr. Green, Darrell's injury was more severe, comparing more closely to the number two cause, gunshot wounds, strictly because of his velocity of impact.

It was a new world for the entire group. Looking back, Darrell realizes how much it meant to have had so much support in those early days.

"As a Christian, my relationship with God was very important through all this," Darrell says. "I went through the 'Why me? Why not me?' And the 'Why not me?' came from having a relationship with God. Most people just ask 'Why me?' over and over again, but when you have a relationship with the man upstairs,

you learn to say 'Why not me?'

"But I don't think I could have gotten through this with just my relationship with God or just with the support of my family and friends," Darrell adds. "It was a combination of all of it that helped me make it through."

Darrell's support network of friends and family never gave him the opportunity to feel sorry for himself, and they made sure someone was with him at all times. Jim Henegar, Darrell's neighbor and friend, visited Jackson every single day Darrell was there.

"I was never alone in my room—not once," Darrell says. "You could never tell how many people were going to be there. We broke every visitor rule you could possibly break. Even when I tried to take a nap, someone would walk in after traveling to see me and say 'Hey, we're here. Wake your ass up.'

"But it also got to be a little overwhelming at times, as Lisa and I had virtually no private time," Darrell continues. "We even had my dad repair the lock on the hospital room door so that Lisa and I could have some time to ourselves for a few minutes."

A sign on Darrell's wall proved to be added motivation: "Tough times never last, but tough people do."

Lisa continued to be Darrell's strength, working as a lab technician a few buildings away during the day and staying with Darrell at night in a bed provided by the hospital.

"I know I have to be strong for him," she said in a *Miami Herald* article written soon after their return. "Crying in his face is not going to help him get better. I go off and cry by myself. I've never shed a tear in front of him."

Lisa was frustrated at times by what she felt was unwarranted praise, but despite her insistence that she wasn't doing anything

ABOVE: A newspaper graphic in *USA Today* explains Darrell's surgery. The goal was to give Darrell a little more control of his right wrist.

"It was unlike anything I had ever experienced," Hawley recalls. "It was as if someone stuck a pin in a balloon and everyone's emotions let loose at once."

special, she was. According to both Dr. Green and Dr. Lasher, anywhere between 75 and 90 percent of marriages that are affected by serious spinal cord injuries end as a result of the difficulties the injuries bring to family life. The doctors say it is nearly unheard of that a patient and an unmarried partner stay together for any length of time after the recovery.

But any hopes of a November wedding slipped away, as the family simply had no time to make plans. "It wasn't like there was ever a conscious decision to call off the wedding," Lisa says. "It was more like it just slipped away. There were so many things going on. Planning a wedding was never even talked about."

Despite the emotional blow, the race team rallied behind the Gwynns, determined to finish Darrell's quest for a championship. Having missed three national events since the Easter Sunday accident, the Coors Extra Gold dragster was back on the track for the first time in early June.

"To see my friend of many years lying in hospital bed probably never being able to walk again—I was ready to quit racing right then," crew chief Ken Veney says. "If tuning Darrell's car was just a job, I would have walked away from the sport the day he crashed. But I realized that he needed me. He needed to have confidence that someone was with his race car making sure it kept getting down the track. He needed that car out there to give him something to fight for. He needed the race team to keep going."

The car had been adjusted to Hawley's size and preferences, but despite plans to test the car before race day, time ran out before Frank got a single pass in Darrell's car. His initial chance to get a feel for his new ride came in the first qualifying run at Columbus. "With all the attention we were receiving, it was very distracting," Hawley says. "But once I sat in the car and talked with Ken [Veney], it became a very natural feeling. This was a race team, this was a race car, and I was at a race. Everything else faded away."

The lack of a test session proved to be no problem for the new

driver and Darrell's crew as the Coors Extra Gold team qualified number one, with a run of 5.043 seconds at 275.98 mph.

As eliminations got underway, Darrell anxiously awaited race results in his hospital room. Jerry called and provided updates after each round. "One down, three to go," Jerry said into the phone after Hawley got a free pass in round one when Wayne Bailey was a no-show.

"Two down, two to go," was the second call, as Hawley overpowered Chris Karamesines 5.066 to 5.209.

"Three down, one to go," Jerry said on the third call, with the team moving past Don Prudhomme and into the finals against Joe Amato.

"I made a phone call to my wife and said 'We're in the finals against Amato,'" Hawley says. "That's when all the 'what ifs' started popping into my head and I started to fantasize a little bit." Amato, the number two qualifier, had scored the low ET (elapsed time) of the round, and was quickest in the first two rounds with runs of 5.090 and 5.062.

When Jerry's final call came, Frank was the winner. Tears began flowing on both ends of the phone.

"It was a mixture of cries," Darrell says. "A cry like we knew we could do it. A cry of happiness. A cry of sadness. And a cry for this being what would have been my best opportunity to win a Top Fuel championship and the fact that I had screwed it up in England."

"It was unlike anything I had ever experienced," Hawley recalls. "It was as if someone stuck a pin in a balloon and everyone's emotions let loose at once." Hawley knocked off Amato 5.122 to 5.221. In just its first race back after Darrell's crash, the team was back in the winner's circle. Darrell knew he had made the right decision in keeping the team together.

Longtime NHRA television announcer Steve Evans recognized the significance of the moment. He ignored his news-gathering instincts, pulled the television cameraman away from the area, and

gave the team several minutes to celebrate before approaching for an emotional interview.

"If you were not a believer in any kind of god, that day would have changed your mind," Veney says. "We didn't do anything special. It just felt like there was someone looking out for us all day."

With all questions about the team answered, Darrell continued to work on his health in Miami. By July, he was doing up to four hours of physical and occupational therapy each day. It was some of those early tasks that Darrell found the most difficult and the most frustrating.

His right arm in a splint, Darrell was forced to begin retraining his muscles to do simple movements. Lowering a spoon into a cereal bowl, the task was to scoop up a Cheerio and direct it to his mouth. Time after time, Darrell would scoop, lift, lose his balance, and start over. Scoop, lift, miss. Scoop, lift, miss.

He finally got the Cheerio to his mouth—a week later.

Other tasks took just as long: reaching for a cookie, writing his name, picking up pegs and putting them in a box. Combined with simple, repetitive stretching movements, there were exercises to work on his eye-to-hand coordination, exercises to help him recline,

and exercises to help him twist his shoulders.

"The therapists were wonderful and they took special pride in helping to develop splints that let me sign autographs," Darrell says. "They knew how important it was for me to keep doing that, and they took special time to help me get it done."

Then Darrell finally got to enjoy one of life's simple pleasures: part of his occupational therapy was learning to take a shower in a special shower chair. "I hadn't had a shower in nearly three months," Darrell said. "I had been washed and kept clean, but I was still feeling grungy. For a guy who used to take at least two showers a day, going three months without one felt nasty."

The tests and adjustments continued as Darrell searched for ways to be more independent. "One of the therapists told me early on that I would learn things every day for the rest of my life that would make things easier and improve my quality of life," Darrell says. "More than twelve years since the accident and that still holds true to this day. I find myself seeking out other quads, sharing tricks I have learned with them, and hoping they have some tricks that will help me."

As Darrell's recovery and education continued, get-well wishes

TOP LEFT: Frank Hawley, left, delivers a storybook win under emotional circumstances when he returned Darrell's car to the track at Columbus. Crew chief Ken Veney and Jerry help surround the trophy. (Auto Imagery)
ABOVE: Friends and family gather for the first Darrell Gwynn Golf Classic, another source of fund-raising. The tournament continues to this day. (Darrell Gwynn collection)

continued to come in from the most unexpected places. From pop singer Michael Jackson to Prime Minister Margaret Thatcher, from Lee Iacocca to President George Bush, special cards kept Darrell's spirit up. "There were a lot of bigwigs coming in and out," says Messina, who continues to be Darrell's main physical therapist. "And Darrell was always smiling and cracking jokes. He inspired the rest of us."

But, as Dr. Lasher noted upon meeting Darrell, he always was well aware of the challenges he was facing. In an article in *USA Today*, Darrell said: "The Miami Project won't be able to perform any miracles and make me a new person, but they are doing what they can. As far as walking at this time, it would be pretty tough."

Says Dr. Green: "Darrell is a winner. A loser who is paralyzed remains a loser. The injury does not transform people into winners. Darrell was a champion and a winner before he was ever in a wheelchair, and the injury didn't change that. He has the spirit of a competitor."

In the early stages of the healing process, Darrell set one primary goal that he really wanted to reach. Scribbling on a piece of paper while trying to relearn to write his name, he penned "DARRELL . . . DARRELL GWYNN . . . LISA . . . MIAMI PROJECT . . . U.S. NATIONALS."

The defending champion of drag racing's most prestigious event and the holder of an ET record (4.90 seconds) that would stand for more than a year after his accident, Darrell wanted to be healthy enough to return to Indy the first week in September. As the U.S. Nationals got closer, Darrell was allowed to make weekend day trips home, eventually working up to an overnight stay. Jerry and a few family friends made sure the family house, and Darrell's townhouse were adjusted for easier living.

"We built a lot of ramps for him to get around our house," Jerry recalls. "At his place, we had to tear out the bathroom and build a new one that he could use."

But going home proved difficult.

"Those early trips just tore me to pieces," Darrell says. "They tore me up big time. Knowing I had to go back to that hospital room was so difficult. I was so selfish at the time about wanting to get out of the hospital that, when I look back, I really inconvenienced some people. My family had to jump through hoops to get me situated."

In an interview with *National Dragster* in August, Darrell was asked: "What do you think of in bed now?"

Darrell responded: "I try to think of what the next five years are going to be like. I was always in perfect health, maybe a cold once a year. I just don't want to be plagued with setbacks. I want to go on with my life after I get out of this hospital. Even though I'm going to feel like I am hurt every day when I can't get out of bed by myself, I'm just praying for a life without further setbacks."

As Indy approached, only one major obstacle remained. Darrell didn't have a proper wheelchair for the trip. The drag racing community came through again, as friends Greg and Mike Peek from the Peek Brothers race team offered to pick up the expense whenever Darrell was ready. With the help of Sunrise Medical and Quickie Wheelchair, Darrell's new ride was overnighted to Jackson.

"It was the biggest, ugliest, safest wheelchair you could put yourself in," Darrell says. "It was the perfect chair for someone in my condition, but I wanted no part of it. I was looking for something a little sleeker, a little racier, and a little less bulky. When it showed up, I said I'd stay home rather than go to Indy in that chair."

Darrell, not wanting to seem ungrateful, called the staff at Quickie and asked for something "a little more streamlined—something that doesn't make me look like I'm hurt so bad. Something that makes me look like I'm still Darrell."

The second chair, overnighted to the lobby of the Adams Mark hotel in Indy, was perfect. Not quite able to sit up on his own, Darrell would have to be double-belted into the wheelchair.

So, set to go despite his doctors being "worried sick," Darrell was

temporarily discharged and headed to Indianapolis along with Jerry, Joan, Lisa, and close friend and crew member Tony Mills. Mills was a Florida paramedic and a real comfort to have nearby.

"Comparing how I travel today with that first trip to Indy, it's a miracle something didn't happen," Darrell says. "With all the transferring on and off of planes and in and out of vans, no one was fully trained to do all that properly. We didn't have a blood pressure cuff or emergency medicines. Heck, we didn't even have a real wheelchair until I got to Indy."

At the last minute, Dr. Green decided to join the family for the trip.

"We were all very nervous," Jerry says. "But, when Dr. Green decided to join us, it gave everyone a little more security with the decision."

Back at the track for the first time since his accident, Darrell was at home with the smells of burning rubber and nitromethane, the cheers from the grandstands, and the smiles from friends he hadn't seen in months.

Joan, however, noticed something a little different.

"You could see the pain in people's faces," Joan says. "Some people were avoiding eye contact because they didn't know what to say or how to react. I remember Darrell saying 'Mom, I don't want them to treat me any different.'"

"My mom was very instrumental in my positive outlook after the injury," Darrell says. "She reminded me that I had a lot of friends and family that loved me and if I just kept being who I was, they would all continue to treat me the same way. She told me to be myself and that's what I've tried to do.

"A lot of my motivation comes from not wanting to let people down. My parents. My friends," he continues. "A lot of my closest friends didn't know how to handle seeing me in a wheelchair without my arm, so it was important to me to make things as easy as possible for everyone and that meant laughing a lot and trying to be the same person I was before the crash."

Lynn Prudhomme tells of her husband's discomfort with the

TOP LEFT: Dr. Barth Green joins Darrell and Lisa at a press conference in Indianapolis just prior to the U.S. Nationals. (Les Welch) **ABOVE RIGHT:** Darrell presents Joyce Schultz with an award at the Car Craft awards ceremony, thanking her for her tireless efforts in coordinating many of the fund-raising efforts for Darrell's recovery. (Darrell Gwynn collection)

BELOW: Darrell's friend Mike Rushlow welcomes his favorite driver back to the track, posting a banner on the side of the family camper. (Darrell Gwynn collection) **RIGHT:** Family friend Don Ness built this special trailer to parade Darrell down the track at Indy. Although it would be used only once, the trailer was carefully planned and beautifully constructed. "They could have put bicycle wheels on a box and thrown me in it," says Darrell, "but not Don Ness." (Darrell Gwynn collection)

moment. "I don't think Don knew what to do," Lynn says. "He didn't really know what to say—he didn't know how to touch Darrell."

One fan, however, knew just how Darrell felt. The pair had met a few years earlier at the 1987 U.S. Nationals when Darrell noticed a young man in a wheelchair cooking in the Indy summer sun outside of the Gwynns' pit area.

"Darrell had waved us into his tent and brought his mom and dad over to meet my son," recalls Don Rushlow, whose son Mike suffers from cerebral palsy. "It was like they couldn't do enough for us. They gave us hats and shirts and pins. They greeted us with such open arms. It was overwhelming."

Instant fans, the Rushlows continued to make the 280-mile trek to Indy each year from their home in Monroe, Michigan, to cheer

for Darrell and his race team, each time joining the Gwynns in their pit area.

In 1989, the year before Darrell's accident, Mike worked around the speech restrictions that come with cerebral palsy and gave Darrell a special computer voice message through a machine attached to his wheelchair. Mike typed in a few letters and pushed a button as Darrell was getting suited up for his final-round U.S. Nationals matchup with Dick LaHaie. The message was simple: "Kick ass!"

Darrell did.

So, when Darrell returned to Indy in a wheelchair of his own, one of the first things he saw was a banner prepared by the Rushlows.

Darrell rolled up to Mike and greeted his old friend.

"Isn't this something?" Darrell said.

Despite the painful irony, Darrell was thrilled to be back at the racetrack.

"It was way cool getting back out there," Darrell says. "Not all my friends could make it to the hospital and I was looking forward to seeing so many people. But it was the fans that made Indy special. The warm welcome they gave me was unforgettable."

Darrell's friend Don Ness coordinated the construction of a special canopied trailer, designed to be pulled behind a golf cart.

"This thing had a chrome suspension. It was badass," Darrell recalls. "And Don and the guys at his shop built this thing knowing its only use was probably going to be a single 1/4-mile pass during prerace ceremonies. They could have put bicycle wheels on a box and thrown me in it, but not Don Ness."

[119]

On Sunday, Darrell rolled his wheelchair onto the trailer and made a pass down the 1/4 mile, with Ness behind the wheel of the cart. The gesture drew a standing ovation and proved to be Darrell's opportunity to say thank you for all the support he had received during his recovery.

At about the same moment, Darrell had a pair of banners flown over the track. A special one for Lisa: "Thanks, I love you." And another for fans and family: "You're the best."

The obvious sentimental favorite to win the race, Darrell parked his chair outside the concrete retaining wall for each round, watching intently as his car moved through the field. The fairy tale ended one round short with a loss to Joe Amato in the final.

On the way back to Miami, Darrell realized the trip to Indy had been the best thing for him and the worst thing for him all at the same time.

"It was great to be back out there with all my friends and to be around the car and the team," Darrell says. "But it was an emotional experience and it reminded me of all I had lost. Going back to the hospital was so difficult."

Two weeks later, however, Darrell would find another excuse to temporarily check out of rehab for a few days. Darrell's former teammate, Kenny Bernstein, had led a charge to put together a benefit softball game to be played in Reading, Pennsylvania, site of the upcoming Keystone Nationals. The game would match NHRA all-stars against another star-studded group from NASCAR. At the time, Bernstein was president of the Professional Racers and Owners Organization (PRO) and a NASCAR Winston Cup Series team owner as well. The circle track guys were at nearby Dover, Delaware, for the Peak 500 and jumped at the chance to help out.

"The softball game was the *Reading Eagle* writer John Ernesto's idea—we just ran with it," Kenny says. "I made some calls to some of the key drivers in NASCAR and they all wanted to help. I remember Earnhardt's response to this day—'I wanna help. We'll play some ball.'"

The softball game was the home run the drag racing community had been searching for.

"There had been a lot of fund-raising at the track and we would get a few thousand dollars each time," says Sheryl Bernstein. "We knew we couldn't keep going back and doing that over and over again. We knew we had to come up with one big event that everyone could put all their focus into."

By the time Bernstein and his gang were finished, sixty-five

ABOVE: In his role as a reporter for NBC Sports, Don Garlits welcomes Darrell back to Indy. (Les Welch) **TOP RIGHT:** Darrell and Jerry watch Frank Hawley at Indy. "Going back to the track was the best thing for me and the worst thing for me all at the same time," says Darrell. (Les Welch)

"The people I know in racing don't like to think about the big crash,"
Rusty Wallace says. "And seeing Darrell in that condition was difficult because it reminded all of us of what can happen in our sport."

drivers were signed up to par-
ticipate.

"The racing family is a tight
family," says NASCAR driver
Rusty Wallace. "It's not like
we all go out to dinner or hang
around each other away from
the track, but if a driver goes
down, the rest of us will show
up in droves to do what we
can to help. That was definitely
a night we all wanted to be there. Darrell was one of our buddies and
we wanted to be there for him."

The Darrell Gwynn Benefit Softball Challenge lineup sheets read
like a who's who of American motor sports.

The NHRA side wore red and sported names like Bernstein, John
Force, Don Prudhomme, Dick LaHaie, Kenny Koretsky, Scott
Kalitta, and Dan Pastorini, with Shirley Muldowney, Gary Ormsby,
and Amato leading a loaded cheering section.

On the NASCAR side, Wallace, Dale Earnhardt, Davey Allison,
Ricky Rudd, Kyle Petty, Bill Elliott, Ernie Irvan, and Mark Martin
were among the drivers to don blue jerseys and make the trip. Not
to be left out, NASCAR brass, including Bill France and Les
Richter, joined NHRA president and coach Dallas Gardner to lend
their support.

Backed by the local newspapers, the *Reading Eagle* and the
Reading Times, in a town Darrell considered his second home after
spending so many summers with Carl Ruth, the game was played
on September 13 at Reading Municipal Stadium, home of the
Philadelphia Phillies AA squad. The minor league baseball facility seated about 7,200, but 15,000 showed up, including more
than a hundred journalists.

Once the record crowd settled in, the festivities started with

Darrell's race team presenting its fallen leader with a birthday cake
as thousands stood to sing "Happy Birthday." All eyes were on
Darrell as he rolled to the mound, lifted his partially paralyzed right
arm, and threw out the first pitch.

"You looked over and saw all those tough ol' NASCAR hillbillies
lined up before the game, and there wasn't a dry eye when Darrell
threw out that first pitch," says Force, who played catcher that
night. "That moment was bigger than any world championship and
everyone knew it. It's one thing to fight and beat the competition on
the racetrack, but when all of these people rallied together from
every category to do this for Darrell, that was something else.
Sometimes you've got to reverse the puzzle of life and look at things
differently. It was quite an experience."

"The people I know in racing don't like to think about the big
crash," Wallace says. "And seeing Darrell in that condition was
difficult because it reminded all of us of what can happen in our sport.
But Darrell is such a cool guy. He's a winner with a great demeanor,
and it was great to see him back out there. He wasn't going to be out
of sight, out of mind."

When it was time to play the game, NASCAR opened with a

RIGHT: Team NHRA surrounds Darrell at the benefit softball game
between NHRA drivers and NASCAR drivers. The game, attended by
15,000 fans and more than 100 journalists, was a huge success and raised
more than $150,000. (Les Welch) **ABOVE:** Former teammate Kenny
Bernstein, reigning NASCAR champion Rusty Wallace, and Darrell share a
few laughs at the game. Bernstein was a key figure in organizing the
fund-raiser. (Les Welch)

"I told him to bring a bunch of garbage bags and get to the hospital as fast as he could," Darrell recalls. "When he got there, I told him to take whatever was in the room, whether it was cards, flowers, clothes, shampoo, whatever. I just wanted to get the hell out of there."

scoreless first inning, and Jerry Gwynn took the first at bat for his son, flying out to left field. The NHRA jumped to an early lead, scoring four runs in their half of the first, highlighted by a Dan Pastorini home run.

Although major league baseball scouts would have been amused at the level of play, the competition was fierce. And when the NASCAR drivers came to bat in the second, Force began what would turn into an evening of constant chatter from his crouched position behind the batter's box.

Not everyone found Force's antics entertaining. By the seventh inning, with NASCAR leading 13-11, Chad Little rounded third and was charging hard toward home. Cheered on by his teammates, Little lowered his shoulder and plowed Force at the plate with a little extra zeal.

"I got up ready to fight and headed toward their dugout," Force recalls. "Then I saw those guys stand up and thought 'This isn't a real good idea.' But I guess all that energy stayed with me because I've only hit two home runs in my entire life—one in the seventh grade after a foul ball broke my girlfriend's nose and the second one in the next inning of that game."

As Darrell and Lisa looked on, the NHRA tied the game at 16 at the end of eight innings, behind Force's homer and hits by Pastorini, LaHaie, and Koretsky. But the NASCAR drivers came out swinging in the ninth. With the bases loaded, Michael Waltrip crushed a grand slam home run to left field.

It appeared that the guys who turned left for a living would have the last laugh.

Down 20-16 heading into the bottom of the ninth, the NHRA took advantage of NASCAR pitcher Ernie Irvan's wildness, mixing a few hits with three walks to load the bases for Koretsky. The Pro Stock driver smacked a line-drive single to left center, scoring a pair of runners and giving the NHRA, and Darrell, a 21-20 victory. The final numbers for both teams: forty-one runs on forty-five

hits and ten errors.

"When I got home that night, I felt like someone had beaten me up," Force adds. "But at the end, through all the bumps and bruises, just to know that we were able to pack the house for such a good thing was special."

When the money was counted, the event had raised more than $150,000 toward Darrell's recovery and care.

"It was an electric evening," Darrell says. "To this day, people come up to me and say 'You don't know me, but I was at the softball game.' It was a magical night."

The next day, a story ran in the *Reading Times*, quoting Muldowney and putting things in perspective: "There's not another Darrell Gwynn out there. We have some young people coming up, but they don't have the style, the charisma, the niceness about them. They're all nice people, but they're not Darrell Gwynn."

When Darrell returned to Miami, it took only another day or two before he decided he was ready to leave the hospital for good. In tears, he called Tony Mills, begging for help getting home. Darrell was due to be discharged November 9, but he couldn't wait another second.

"I told him to bring a bunch of garbage bags and get to the hospital as fast as he could," Darrell recalls. "When he got there, I told him to take whatever was in the room, whether it was cards, flowers, clothes, shampoo, whatever. I just wanted to get the hell out of there. Whether it was right or wrong, I knew I couldn't stay there another minute. I knew it was selfish, but I was going crazy."

Tony obliged and the pair made their escape.

"There was no fear in going home," Darrell says. "From the time of the accident, the goal was always to get back home, to sleep in my own bed, and to get back into as much of my life's routine as possible. I think other people were worried, but my only fear was staying in that hospital one more day."

TOP LEFT: Darrell throws the first pitch to open the game. (NHRA, *National Dragster*) BELOW: The box score from the ball game—a veritable who's who of racing. (NHRA, *National Dragster*) BOTTOM LEFT: Darrell poses with funny car legend John Force, who slammed a home run in the ball game. (Darrell Gwynn collection)

NHRA

	AB	R	H	BI	BB
Gwynn c	1	0	0	0	0
Bernstein ss	6	1	2	2	0
Johnson cf	5	3	2	0	1
Hendey 1b	3	1	1	0	2
Pastorini rvr	5	3	2	4	1
Kalitta S. 3b,cf		3	1	0	1
Koretsky 2b	5	0	3	3	0
LaHaie rf	4	1	2	4	0
White p	1	0	0	0	1
Oswald lf	2	2	1	0	0
Force c	3	2	2	2	1
Hartman 3b	2	2	1	2	1
Head 2b	2	1	0	0	0
Neely cf	1	1	1	1	0
Prudhomme p	2	1	0	0	1
Grose rf	1	0	0	0	0
TOTAL	47	21	18	18	9

NASCAR

	AB	R	H	BI	BB
Petty K. cf	6	3	3	0	0
O'Neil rvr	4	3	4	0	0
Allison D. 1b	6	2	4	3	0
Irvan p	6	2	2	2	0
Cope c	4	0	0	1	2
Bodine G. lf	3	1	2	0	0
Wilson 2b	5	1	1	0	1
Waltrip M. rf	6	3	4	6	0
Bodine B. 3b	5	2	2	1	0
Martin ss	3	0	0	0	0
Rudd rvr	2	1	1	2	0
Marlin lf	3	2	3	3	0
Little ss	2	0	1	1	0
LaBonte ss	3	0	0	0	0
Schrader 2b	1	0	0	0	0
TOTAL	60	20	27	19	3

WP-Prudhomme, LP-Irvan. E-NHRA (5), NASCAR (5).
2B - Hendey, Koretsky, Irvan (2), Marlin, Petty, Allison, LaHaie (2), Bernstein. 3B - Waltrip, Neely, Marlin. HR - Pastorini, Force, Waltrip. T-2:50. A-15,000.

THE BENCH: NHRA - Gary Ormsby, Joe Amato, Bruce Larson, Ed McCulloch, Frank Hawley, Eddie Hill, Mike Brotherton, Lori Johns, Frank Bradley, Shirley Muldowney, Tom Hoover, K.C. Spurlock, Chuck Etchells, Maurice DuPont, Whit Bazemore, Wayne Bailey, Jerry Caminito, Paul Smith, and Frank Kramberger.

NASCAR - Dale Earnhardt, Rusty Wallace, Bill Elliott, Dave Marcis, Hut Stricklin, Rob Moroso, Greg Sacks, Harry Gant, Bobby Allison, Neil Bonnett, Jimmy Means, Bobby Hillin, Jack Pennington, Dick Trickle, and Morgan Shepherd.

Chapter Eight: Back on Track

In 1991, Darrell's race team headed back to the track with most of its pieces still in place. Frank Hawley took his position behind the wheel, and Ken Veney continued in his role as crew chief. The only noticeable change came as the familiar Coors Extra Gold paint scheme was replaced by the blue and silver colors of the new Coors Light Silver Bullet brand. But despite continued financial support from the growing beer company, the sponsor's enthusiasm for the program was beginning to fade.

"We went back out there, in part, as a favor to Darrell," says Coors executive Steve Saunders. "After the accident, the excitement and the energy were no longer there. We liked Frank and we had some fun with him for a couple of seasons, but things weren't the same."

Early in '91, the Silver Bullet proved less than spectacular at the track. After six races, the freshly painted dragster ventured past the second round just once—a semifinal loss in Phoenix.

At home, Darrell continued his daily rehab, relying on regular physical therapy to keep his idle muscles functioning properly. Exercise and "lots of talking" helped strengthen Darrell's breathing. The deep breaths he needed between sentences shortened in time, and multiple naps became less necessary.

In a May newspaper article, Darrell described one of his physical therapy sessions: "Today was basically stretching my chest, so five years from now I don't end up curled in a ball. The muscles in my chest try to shorten up because I am sitting up so often and the therapists need to stretch me around like a contortionist."

Darrell also attended regular biofeedback sessions at the Miami Project, where sensors were attached to different parts of his body to measure nerve activity in his muscles. At Darrell's first session, the signal between his brain and right triceps muscle measured at 2 percent. Later, readings improved to 14 percent, but remained well below the 50 to 60 percent needed to move the muscle.

At one point, the plan was to fit Darrell with a prosthetic arm, aiding in his independence.

"Early on, we were excited about getting the arm," Darrell recalls. "But I found out they would have to take about four more inches off my arm and I would lose my elbow. It would be fine, if I wore the new arm all the time and everything worked well. But if the arm didn't work well or it was not comfortable, I would have given up my elbow and my balance. I wasn't willing to risk that.

"And even with the arm, the movements were clumsy and difficult. I would have to move my right shoulder to get the left arm to move and then I would have to hit a switch to get the hand to work. It just wasn't worth it." Living with Lisa, Darrell did his best to find a routine he was comfortable with, but there was no hiding the limitations. Getting up in the morning, brushing his teeth, getting a shower, and combing his hair—tasks that took maybe twenty minutes before the accident—now required more than an hour and at least one other person.

On one of the first nights at home in his condo, Darrell was determined to sit with Lisa on a new leather couch the couple had purchased before the accident.

LEFT: With limited funding in 1993, Darrell took on the job of crew chief, but the travel and long hours wore him out. "I just couldn't put in the fifteen to sixteen hours a day a crew chief needs to put in to be successful at this level," Darrell says. (Darrell Gwynn collection) **ABOVE:** Michael Brotherton replaced Frank Hawley behind the wheel of the Gwynn Top Fuel dragster in 1992. (Darrell Gwynn collection)

Not yet fully trained in transferring Darrell in and out of the wheelchair, Lisa was confident she could get Darrell onto the couch.

Once propped on the couch, Darrell was happy and they settled in to watch television. For a few hours, they were back doing what they had done so many times before.

"Then came getting him back in the wheelchair," Lisa says. "He slipped through my hands. I basically dropped him on the floor. And I tried everything I could think of, but I couldn't lift him back into the chair."

"We laughed and cried while she kept trying to lift me back up," Darrell says. "She would try for a while, give up and then try again. She just couldn't lift the dead weight. She tried for hours before I was finally back in the chair.

"People ask me where my motivation comes from—that's where it comes from. I'm lying on the floor staring at my beautiful fiancée and I don't want to lose her. I had already lost enough and I didn't want to lose any more."

All Darrell wanted to do was watch TV on his new couch with his girlfriend. It was just one of many brutal reminders that his life was no longer the same. In many cases, what Darrell wanted to do and what Darrell could do would never come together again.

Some of the couple's biggest challenges, however, were virtually invisible, with something as seemingly inconsequential as an ingrown toenail now a potential killer for Darrell: autonomic dysreflexia, a condition common in spinal cord patients, allows minor irritants that normally cause pain or discomfort to go unnoticed by paralysis victims. Pressure by a foreign object in Darrell's shoe or in his wheelchair, a South Florida sunburn, or an unseen scrape or cut might trigger elevated blood pressure and pounding headaches. Even something as simple as tight or restrictive clothing had the potential to become a medical emergency.

During Darrell's first few months at home, family and friends did their best to handle his daily care. An agency was hired to assist, but Darrell didn't like the medical atmosphere it created.

"It was very impersonal," Darrell recalls. "It was too clinical and too 'no fun' for me. But I didn't know what else to do."

Two months later, Darrell canceled the service and opted for

ABOVE: The Hrudka girls clockwise from bottom left: Lori, Tracey, Trisha, and Jody pose with Darrell at the Springnationals in Columbus, Ohio. The four are the daughters of Tom and Jo Hrudka, founders of the Mr. Gasket company. Mr. Gasket was a supporter throughout Darrell's career. (Darrell Gwynn collection)

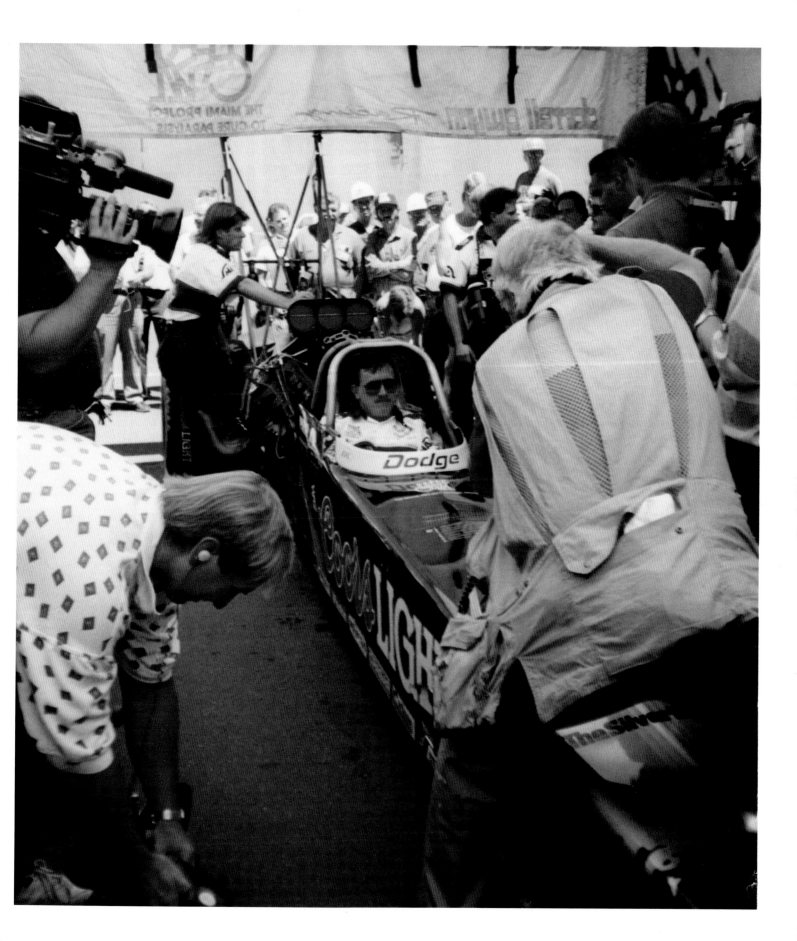

the more personal approach of family and friends. His chosen attendants included Lisa's cousin Dennis Bambach, a fireman/paramedic, and Gwynn crew member Tony Mills, another local fireman who had been called into duty for the first time a year earlier, during Darrell's stay at Jackson.

"I was getting a bath in my shower chair," Darrell recalls. "This woman was washing me gently with a cloth, and as she moved to my private areas, she was just lightly dabbing the cloth. So I yelled in to Tony, 'Hey, get in here and show this woman how to wash a set of balls.' Everyone just broke into laughter and that led to Tony helping with my care. It certainly wasn't something either one of us planned for or something either of us wanted to be doing, but that's how he became my original attendant."

As time went on, additional firemen and paramedics became part of the team. The one-day-on, two-days-off life of emergency workers meant someone was always available to help Darrell and Lisa. Glen Checchi, Tab Williams, Jorge Muvdi, Jarrod Wolf, James Knight, Bobby Soto, Chad Robertson, Jason Bohan, Jeff Robson, Tim Suggs—the list kept growing.

"What's cool about the way things worked out was that these guys all became friends," Darrell says. "We are very close and our families are close. There are very few things I can do for myself. These guys do the rest."

Back at the track, Darrell's crew was exhausted, emotionally and physically. They had not taken a weekend off since before the racing season. With several open weekends between NHRA events following early May's Mid-South Nationals in Memphis, the guys finally took a well-deserved break. Not since Darrell's accident had the team really taken time for themselves.

After working on the car at the Gwynns' Miami garage until late in the afternoon on May 17, mechanics Nick Floch and Gary Clark headed for the Florida Keys to join Chris Hyatt, Rob Flynn, and Michele Flynn at the Hyatt's vacation cottage. They enjoyed a dinner of grilled steak and shrimp, and then the group set out for an evening bayside cruise on the Intercoastal Waterway aboard the Hyatts' 23-foot Seacraft.

Returning home a few hours later, Chris's father, Mike, apparently misjudged the position of an unlighted marker in Tarpon Basin. The collision sent Nick and Gary overboard, both men slamming into the marker. Nick hit his head. Gary lost an arm. Frantically fished from the water and transported to a private dock behind the home of Orlando Castelano in Key Largo, Nick and Gary died at the scene despite the work of dozens of emergency workers.

Nick was twenty-six. Gary was thirty-five.

"I got a call from Rob at about eleven o'clock that night, and he told me there was a bad accident on the boat and I needed to get down there," Jerry says. "We didn't know any details." Picking up a speeding ticket along the way, Jerry and Joan made the 80-mile drive to the address Rob had given Jerry over the phone.

"When we got there, they told us Nick and Gary were already gone," Jerry says. "'Gone to the hospital?' I asked. I couldn't believe they were dead."

Jerry and Joan stayed for a few hours before making the drive back to Miami in the middle of the night. Jerry dropped Joan off at their house and reluctantly made his way to Darrell's condo. "This was something I couldn't tell Darrell over the phone," Jerry says. "You don't tell your son over the phone that two of his best buddies are gone."

Jerry and Nick's father, Bob Floch, raced each other often in the early seventies while Darrell and Nick hung out together in the pits as kids. Gary was also a racer, facing off against both Jerry and Darrell before joining the Gwynns as a crew member. His "jack of all trades" skills were well known around the track and invaluable to the team. "Having Gary on the crew was like having three or four guys, because he knew a little bit about everything," Jerry says. "He was an electrician, a welder—you could bring up any topic and Gary seemed to know something about it."

"And Nick was just the nicest guy in the world," Darrell says. "When Lisa would come to the shop and take me out to lunch, Nick would wash her car and have it all clean when we got back. He was always doing little things like that."

Jerry arrived at Darrell's condo a little before seven o'clock in the morning. Darrell's friend and neighbor, Jim Henegar, heard the knocking and joined the family. "They were banging on the door

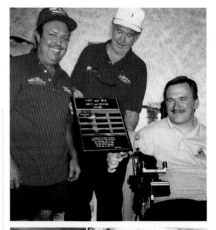

before I had gotten out of bed," Darrell recalls. "Dennis Bambach was there, helping Lisa get me started for the day, when they came back into my bedroom and shared with me all that had happened over the last eight hours.

"We were in total shock," Darrell adds. "To wake up to the news that Nick and Gary were gone— we just sat in the room and cried for hours. As if the last year hadn't been hard enough, now we had this. It was almost too much. I hit bottom when I got hurt, but I hit rock bottom when those two guys died."

Separate funerals were planned in Ohio and South Carolina. Jerry and Joan flew to each, but Darrell was left behind; the logistics needed to get to both events would have been impossible with Darrell still learning his way around in a wheelchair.

After the funerals, despite the heartache, the team decided to keep moving forward. "We were already committed," Darrell says. "We were six races into the season, and with all the bad things Coors had already been through, we couldn't quit." The team, however, needed "instant crew members with instant experience." Darrell rounded up Mike Gerry and former Kenny Bernstein mechanic Doug Kuch, and the team went back to work.

But returning to the track proved difficult for everyone. A simple memorial wreath with "Gary and Nick" on a small ribbon adorned the team's pit entrance. It was anything but business as usual.

ABOVE LEFT: Nick Floch, a crew member and friend, was killed in a boating accident less than a year after Darrell's accident. "I don't know how we went on after this," Darrell recalls. (Darrell Gwynn collection)
ABOVE RIGHT: Gary Clark was the second crew member killed in the same boating accident. (Darrell Gwynn collection)

"A lot of my memories with those two guys and the rest of the team were built around our life on the road," Darrell says. "We had it all at one time, and it felt like piece by piece it was all going away. I don't know how I got through it. But going back to the race shop was the one thing I knew I could do. Racing has always been my security blanket and I needed it more than ever."

Years later, in memory of his fallen friends, Darrell began awarding the Above and Beyond award to members of his race team who exemplified the extra effort that always came from Nick and Gary.

Two months after the boating accident, Darrell and Lisa were rocked with more bad news as Ronnie Hughes suffered a massive heart attack. The Uncle Ronnie who took such pride in bringing the couple together a few years earlier would not live to see their wedding. "I think Ronnie's death was very significant in Darrell's life," Joan says. "They had a very special relationship. I think Darrell gets a lot of his sense of humor from Ronnie. He meant a lot to both Darrell and Lisa. Losing Ronnie hurt everyone."

Trying to avoid a prolonged depression, Darrell once again looked to the people around him at home and at the racetrack. "The inspiration to keep going came from the same support group that helped me get through my accident," Darrell says. "Everyone, including the good Lord, was telling me that good things were going to happen again. I just had to stick with it and have faith that things would turn around."

At Columbus, Frank and the team advanced to the semis before falling to Don Prudhomme, but in the shadow of multiple tragedies, the Silver Bullet ride would fail to find its way to victory circle in 1991. By the end of the season, an option year for Coors, the sponsor was disappointed with the team's performance. Corporate enthusiasm for the program continued to decline.

Further complicating the matter, Frank Hawley decided not to return for the '92 season, opting instead to spend more time tending to his growing drag racing school.

Eventually convincing Coors to return for another season, Darrell turned the wheel over to thirty-six-year-old Michael Brotherton, a relative newcomer to the NHRA Top Fuel ranks. The Oklahoma

ABOVE: The Coors Light Silver Bullet transporter and dragster shining in the South Florida sun. (Darrell Gwynn collection) **RIGHT:** On January 10, 1993—more than two years later than they had planned—Darrell and Lisa were married. Says Lisa, "I think everyone needed the wedding." (Darrell Gwynn collection)

native, a 1990 IHRA Top Fuel champion, not only brought money from associate sponsor Wiltel Communications to the Gwynns, but also sported a marketing degree and a history as a business manager. These were assets the Gwynn team needed, with another sponsor search looming in the near future.

Mike Gerry stayed on with the crew for the '92 season, joining full-timers Rob Flynn, Brian Vanetti, Joe Shaffer, and Chris Cunningham. With Ken Veney still tuning the dragster, the team managed one win in 1992, but the partnership with Brotherton failed in most other areas.

"We had a lot of nice equipment when we started the season," Darrell says. "And not a lot of nice equipment at the end of the year. We had a couple of wrecked race cars and a lot of broken pieces."

By the end of the 1992 season, the future of the team once again was in question. Brotherton would not be returning and, despite pleas from Darrell, neither would Coors. Without money from Coors, the team would not be able to afford Veney.

"I understood Coors' position," Darrell says. "I tried talking them into one more year, but they had invested a lot of money in something they couldn't have anymore. I thought maybe we could fill the void with Frank or Mike, but it just didn't work out. What made it even more difficult was that my relationship with Coors was the best I could ever imagine with a sponsor. I really believe that if I had never been hurt, they'd still be my sponsor today."

So, at the end of 1992, the Darrell Gwynn team that could taste a championship just a few years earlier was without a driver, without a sponsor, and was looking hard to find a way to stay in business.

At home, however, everything was falling into place.

On January 10, 1993, Darrell and Lisa were married at the

Sheridan Hills Baptist Church in Hollywood, Florida. Darrell's father Jerry served as his best man. Lisa's sister, Michelle, was the maid of honor.

"I remember sitting off in a side room waiting for things to begin," says Darrell, who survived a bachelor party that included some combination of hot oil and women wrestlers. "Everyone kept saying, 'This is it. It's finally going to happen.' The only time I can recall being that nervous with anticipation was suiting up for the finals of the U.S. Nationals. I know it's not the same thing, but it's the only way I can describe the butterflies I had in my stomach."

The racing community was well represented, as Garlits, Prudhomme, and Amato were among those in attendance. With nearly four hundred friends and relatives seated in the pews, mothers escorted to the front row, and bridesmaids and groomsmen positioned around the altar in pageantlike fashion, Lisa was delivered

to Darrell's side by her father, Wayne. The couple that had begun as childhood friends repeated their vows and exchanged rings in front of Reverend Bill Billingsley and a packed church. After waiting for more than two years, Darrell and Lisa finally were pronounced husband and wife.

"The wedding was important," Lisa says. "It reminded us we were a couple again. There were times after Darrell's accident when I was feeling like I was just part of the circus that our life had become. And I think everyone was so happy to see that we finally made it after all we had been through."

The reception was held at Pier 66 in Fort Lauderdale, and as the music began for the traditional first dance, the crowd gathered to see how Darrell and Lisa would pull it off. Lisa gathered up her mag-

nificent gown and nestled into her new husband's lap. Darrell maneuvered the chair into a slow spin, and the couple laughed and kissed to the words of Al Jarreau's "So Good."

"There wasn't a dry eye in the house," Lisa says. "We had practiced a little before the wedding, but I still wasn't sure we would be able to do it without running over my dress or something. It was a wonderful moment for everyone." The singing and dancing went on for hours; Jerry even offered to pay the extra fee to keep the band and the bar going beyond midnight.

The race season was only a few weeks away, so a West Coast honeymoon, with stops in Carmel, Monterey, and a beach house in Mendocino, was scheduled for later in the year between events in Denver, Sonoma, and Seattle.

Still looking for a driver, Darrell turned his attention back to the team, placing a phone call to Funny Car standout Mike Dunn. Dunn had raced a few Top Fuel events in 1992 for former major league baseball player and aspiring team owner Jack Clark, and he

[132]

ABOVE: Originally engaged to be married in November of 1990, the couple had to postpone their ceremony for more than two years after the Easter Sunday accident. (Darrell Gwynn collection)

His top speed is 6 mph, but Gwynn holds the driver's seat

GWYNN from A-1

known as "the Kid" became a grim statistic: one of more than 10,000 Americans who are paralyzed every year.

Now, three years later, Gwynn is back in control. These days it's not his foot stomping the gas to blast down a quarter-mile track in less than 5 seconds. It's his mind steering his team back toward victory. He's back in the pits calling the shots. He's the boss, the brainpower, the first professional crew chief to try to make a car run better, quicker, smoother without being able to touch it.

He has plenty of help, plenty of motivation. Veterans advise him. Good friends act as his hands. His fiancee recently became his wife. His parents remain his most unfailing fans. He has a deepening faith in God.

And not least of all, he still has racing. The sport that brought him his deepest pain still gives him his greatest pleasure.

"I'll race forever," Gwynn said. "Maybe not as crew chief — it's too hard on my lifestyle — but I'll always be involved. Racing is my life. It gave me what I had, and what I had keeps me going."

✔ ✔ ✔

The spacious headquarters of Darrell Gwynn Racing grew from a hobby begun by Gwynn's father, Jerry, in the 1950s. Now Dad manages the team. Son owns it.

The speed-limit sign posted in the south Broward County shop reads 300 mph. Once the quickest man on Earth, Gwynn now tops out at 6 mph in his motorized wheelchair. He can move only his head and right arm. Crushed in the accident, his left arm is amputated at the elbow.

The engine that drives his

Darrell Gwynn claims the garter of his bride, Lisa, at their wedding this past January. Love survived the crash. A former Orange Bowl queen, Lisa, 27, works as a medical researcher.

SPECIAL TO THE SENTINEL

comeback is this creed, hanging prominently on the shop wall: "... We cannot change the inevitable. The only thing we can do is play on the one thing we have, and that is our attitude. ... I am convinced that life is 10% of what happens to me and 90% how I react to it ...."

The office is filled with mementos — the plaques, trophies, magazine spreads, headlines — chronicling Gwynn's rise to stardom. He may never climb to the same heights again — glory goes to the driver — but his goals are the same. He's still hungry to win.

"Nothing's changed," said Tony Mills, a part-time teammate and close friend. "Darrell is not in the car anymore, but we can still win. We can do anything we want. Darrell has taught us that."

We can do anything we want. Through example, Gwynn delivers that message not just to his team-

mates but to other victims of spinal-cord injuries.

Even before his accident, the racer chose the Miami Project to Cure Paralysis as a charitable cause to promote at the track. Back then, he was just a celebrity raising awareness. Now he's a major inspiration.

The Miami Project logo is the universal symbol for the disabled — a stick figure in a wheelchair — but with a twist. The stick figure

is rising to its feet. Gwynn added his own touch. The standing figure now wears a racing helmet and holds a checkered flag.

Gwynn travels the nation's race-tracks with that logo plastered on all his equipment. Even for the able-bodied, the National Hot Road Association circuit is rigorous. For Gwynn, simply getting to 20 races a year is hard work. His wheelchair won't fit in airplane aisles. His 6-foot-2, 200-pound body has to be lifted over immobile armrests.

Participating in races often makes him sick. His body's internal thermostat is broken, and he is bundled up on all but the hottest days. Though he could complain about so much more, always being cold is his biggest gripe.

A year after he was paralyzed, Gwynn lost two of his teammates and closest friends in a pleasure-boat accident. Then at the end of the 1992 season, Coors Lite quit sponsoring his team. His driver bailed out.

For the first time, Gwynn considered quitting. At $2,000 or more a run, drag racing is too expensive without a sponsor. It's impossible without a driver.

Then, in a testament to Gwynn's reputation, La Victoria Foods, maker of salsas, agreed to back the team with veteran driver Mike Dunn. When Dunn drove the Gwynn car at the first NHRA race this year, he lost the first round but improved in every succeeding race. Last weekend, he placed second at the Winston Invitational at Rockingham, N.C.

If the past is indicative of the future, the Gwynn team should win the next one. "That's our aim, but, you know, one week the race car runs well; the next week it doesn't," Gwynn said. "There's only one thing consistent in my life."

Her name is Lisa.

✔ ✔ ✔

A hush fell over the reception hall. It was time for the first dance, and everybody wondered how the bride and groom would pull it off. Piling her wedding train in her arms, Lisa Hurst Gwynn jumped into her husband's lap, and, kissing, the couple whirled round and round in his wheelchair.

Ever since Gwynn's accident, Lisa Gwynn, 27 — former Orange Bowl queen and Miss Miami, now a medical researcher at the Miami Project — has had to learn to adjust. She has had to get over her annoyance with people who assumed her life with Gwynn was over.

She had to get over her doubts that it might be.

"We had to start from scratch," she said. "I had to learn to fall in love with the new Darrell."

It was hard work, but Gwynn made it easier. He needed help, but he never wanted pity. He suffered deeply, but he never lost his humor.

"That enhanced my love for him," she said. "The inner Darrell has not changed, and I'm still in love with the inner Darrell. I can't live my life without the inner Darrell. That feeling overpowers everything else."

Lisa. Racing. Friends and family. Winning. All constants from the past that propel Gwynn to the future.

He does not like to dwell on the reason for his new life, but sometimes unanswerable questions tug at the depths of his soul. Sometimes he thinks about all the drivers who have walked away from crashes far worse than his, and he wonders, "Why me?"

The answer comes to him quietly.

"Why not me?"

ABOVE: Always a fisherman, Darrell loves being by the water. (Darrell Gwynn collection) **RIGHT:** Darrell called in friend Ralph Gorr, left, to give him a hand at the Mile High Nationals in Denver. The result was the team's first win with Mike Dunn, right, and sponsor La Victoria. It was also Darrell's first win as a crew chief. (Darrell Gwynn collection)

thought he might be able to bring some money to the team.

"Mike and I had grown up around the sport in similar fashion," Darrell says. "We knew each other from being around the tracks together, and he already was among the best Funny Car drivers in the sport. He had driven a Top Fuel car for Jack, so I knew he already had some seat time and would be very capable."

Mike, the first Funny Car driver to break the 280-mph barrier, was in the middle of a sponsor search of his own when Darrell called. "I talked to about five or six companies before I even talked to Darrell, so I decided to call them all back and let them know we were teaming up," Mike says. "One of those companies was La Victoria."

The Southern California salsa company liked the idea and was willing to commit $300,000 to the program. Combined with Darrell's strong associate sponsors, however, the team would start with a budget of nearly $600,000 in 1993. Darrell Gwynn Racing was back in business.

The only missing piece of the puzzle was someone to make the tuning decisions. "We didn't really have enough money to hire Veney back, so I decided I would do it myself," Darrell says. "I figured I wasn't that rusty and I had been doing a little bit of it before my accident." Very few questioned his credentials.

"Darrell knew every piece of that race car," says friend Ralph Gorr. "You could take apart the entire race car and put all the pieces in a pile and Darrell would have no trouble putting it back together."

The move required some adjustments. Since the team's hauler was not wheelchair accessible, Jerry designed and built a special box on the outside of the trailer that housed the computer. Now Darrell could view the data on every 1/4-mile pass without having to find his way into the trailer.

The new driver—crew chief combination worked, and the team put together a competitive season, finishing fourth in the Winston points race, ahead of teams piloted by Joe Amato, Ed McCulloch,

Cory McClenathan, and Don Prudhomme. Mike won his first career Top Fuel event at the Mopar Parts Mile High Nationals at Colorado's Bandimere Speedway and picked up a second win, five events later, at the Chief Auto Parts Nationals at the Texas Motorplex. In addition, the team made three more final-round appearances, including one at the Winston Invitational.

Darrell Gwynn Racing was winning again, but the physical demands of running the team and making the decisions at every race began to take their toll. "It literally wore my ass out," Darrell says. "Going to every single race was a challenge. I think finishing fourth in points and winning a couple of races in my first year with Mike was quite an accomplishment."

In early November, Darrell and Lisa bought a piece of land west of Fort Lauderdale in the community of Weston and went to work designing a home friendlier to Darrell's condition—one that had plenty of room for children.

Lisa had been accepted to medical school and began meeting with

fertility doctors at the Miami Project to discuss the possibility of having a baby with Darrell. "We both had children on the brain," Darrell recalls. "We were living in a 1,200-square-foot condo, and we were ready to start building our dream house. Part of that dream included room for live-in help. Part of that dream included children."

As the 1994 race season approached, Darrell once again assumed crew chief duty, but this time the setup got away from him early in the season. He was physically exhausted as the La Victoria dragster failed to make it past the second round in any of the first nine events.

"I just couldn't put in the fifteen- and sixteen-hour days that I could before my accident," Gwynn says. "And those are the kind of hours crew chiefs have to put in to be successful, so I felt like I was holding the team back. It was time to get someone else in there."

There was little talent available for mid-season pickup, but the team needed some basic help. Darrell hired well-traveled former racer Frank Bradley. The transition was anything but smooth. Bradley's surly demeanor made him few friends in the Gwynn camp, but he was successful in turning the team around.

"They called crew chief Tim Richards 'the General,' so we called Frank 'the Führer,'" Mike recalls. "There was no compromising with Frank Bradley. I grew up in that kind of environment so I really didn't have a problem with it, but there is no doubt Frank could be difficult." By season's end, Mike was once again piloting a stout hot rod, setting career bests in elapsed time and speed at the Winston Select Finals.

Despite the obvious benefit of Frank's efforts, Darrell wasn't used to the volatile atmosphere in the pit area. Even a seventh-place finish in points and a competitive car had too high a price tag, as Bradley fired several members of Darrell's crew, including longtime family friend Chris Cunningham.

"Even if we had won every race, putting up with Frank almost wouldn't have been worth it," Darrell says. "It was that difficult. Frank

was a time bomb. If you said the wrong thing, he would throw shit and walk out.

"It was even more difficult because I really respected what Frank could do on the racetrack," Darrell adds. "As a kid, I was a fan of Frank Bradley."

At home, things were becoming nearly as complicated. "When we needed support, it was great to have so many people around," Lisa says. "But there were times when I really struggled with our lack of privacy. I felt like just another caregiver. I wasn't Darrell's wife. So much of our life was happening in front of other people."

Counseling helped the couple work through the transition. Darrell needed to be reminded that Lisa still needed him as much as he had needed her.

"There were a lot of little things I physically couldn't do anymore to make Lisa feel special," Darrell says. "I couldn't hold her hand or put my arm around her shoulder. I learned I had to be more creative. I had to come up with new ways to make Lisa feel special." In a magazine article entitled "How We Make Our Marriage Work," Darrell explained: "I can bring her flowers or call her at work to find out how she's doing. I learned the littlest things can make her happy."

Trying to juggle his responsibilities at home and at the race shop, Darrell could only laugh when he read Frank Bradley's contract proposal for the 1995 season.

"It was the most ridiculous contract I had ever seen in my life," Darrell says. "It had all sorts of protection for Frank and absolutely none for Darrell Gwynn Racing. I guess he had been screwed so many times in previous relationships that he just went overboard with this one. He made sure he had a contract that covered him from here to the moon."

Darrell and Jerry brought in the team's lawyers to negotiate with Frank.

"Frank walked into the room, looked around, and crudely said, 'Something smells like piss in here,'" Darrell says. "We all just

ABOVE: Victory lane at the Mile High Nationals. "It was a big deal because it was Mopar's event and they were an associate sponsor with us. The president and vice president of marketing of La Victoria were there. It was a great win for our program," Darrell says. (Darrell Gwynn collection)

looked at each other. Then he said, 'Must be those lawyers.' Nobody knew what to say, and Frank just sat there with absolutely no plans to alter the deal in any way."

Despite Darrell's efforts to have Frank work through changes in the contract, Bradley remained firm. With no other qualified crew chiefs available in the Gwynn's price range, Darrell gave in and reluctantly signed Bradley to tune the car in 1995.

The team again performed well under Bradley's wrenching, winning the Slick 50 Nationals in Houston, the Autolite Nationals in Sonoma, California, and the Champion Auto Stores Nationals in Brainerd, Minnesota. At Brainerd, Mike qualified number one and scored low ET and top speed of the event. With a pair of runner-up finishes to add to their credit, Darrell Gwynn Racing finished fourth in the championship race.

ABOVE: Darrell and his family rebuilt the car that crashed at Santa Pod, using many of the original pieces. It is now on display in the Don Garlits Museum of Drag Racing in Ocala, Florida. "We had so many pieces to the car that it made sense to put it back together," says Darrell. "As painful as it was to do, it was a lot of fun too." (Auto Imagery)

BELOW: Darrell and Lisa with friends Chad Robertson and Cheryl Varner at the David Letterman Show. "He was nice enough to take time after the show to spend some time with us," Darrell recalls. (Darrell Gwynn collection) **TOP RIGHT:** As a wedding gift, Lisa gave Darrell a black lab they named Checkers, but both of them wanted an even bigger family and began working with fertility experts at the Miami Project in hopes of having children. (Darrell Gwynn collection)

At home, Darrell and Lisa broke ground on their new home, but learned their desire to have children was not going to be without its difficulties. The medications Darrell used every day to prevent infections might be leaving him virtually sterile. In addition, Joan had confided in Lisa years earlier that while pregnant with Darrell, she had taken a medication to prevent miscarriages that later was linked to infertility in the respective children.

"There was a real fear that we might not be able to have children," Lisa says. "We weren't sure—and neither were the doctors—if it was a temporary condition due to the medicines or something more long-standing and permanent." It would take monthly visits and several adjustments to his medications before they got an answer: Darrell had the "swimmers" necessary to hope for a pregnancy. "When we finally saw them, it was an awesome, awesome event," Lisa says.

As the team prepared for the 1996 season, internal disagreements at La Victoria led to its withdrawal from racing and forced Darrell to once again prepare for a sponsor search. But this time there was a quick replacement. Mopar Parts, an associate sponsor with Darrell since 1986, stepped up to back the team.

The Frank Bradley era, however, came to an end six races into the '96 season after a tuning disagreement in Atlanta led to his clean break from the team. Darrell turned to old friend Ken Veney to help the team get through the rest of the season. There was no complicated contract, simply a race-by-race handshake agreement. "Ken agreed to help us until the end of the season, but after only a few races, I knew this was the guy I wanted to work with," Mike recalls.

The 1996 season ended with one win—Memphis—and a seventh-place finish in the point standings.

Chapter Nine:
Miracles and Memories

A s 1997 got underway, Jerry, Harvey Collins, Bob Bridges, and several other family friends were putting the finishing touches on Darrell and Lisa's new 4,300-square-foot South Florida home.

Local contractors wandered by, impressed with the quality of work being done on the canal-front corner lot. "We got to know a lot of the other builders in the development," says Jerry, who did much of the work on the house with his friends. "They were impressed with how we were putting it together. They told us they'd never make any money if they built to our standards."

The house was completed on February 11. Darrell, Lisa, and their black lab, Checkers, a wedding gift from Lisa to Darrell, moved in three days later—Valentine's Day.

Designed with electric doors and expansive open areas to make Darrell's movements easier, the new home had three bedrooms and plenty of room for live-in help on one side; a large living area, dining area, kitchen, and office in the middle; and a master bedroom and bath with a shower that made getting ready in the morning easier for everyone.

"We looked at sixteen different floor plans and narrowed it down to the three or four we liked best," Darrell says. "From those plans, we took the features we liked the most from each and went to an architect with our ideas."

Phones, intercoms, and switches were installed within Darrell's reach and an enclosed patio area, highlighted by a beautiful pool and spa, included ramps for easy access. Darrell was on-site daily, making decisions about everything from where walls would be built to the color of door hinges.

To help with interior comfort, the house was designed with three heating and cooling units, allowing for slightly different temperature zones in the house. In the summer, the master bedroom and bath remain warmer than the rest of the house to help keep Darrell's body temperature at a comfortable level. The middle of the house is set a few degrees cooler and the guest end of the house a few degrees cooler still.

Settling into their new home, the couple's attention soon turned back to children, as Darrell and Lisa continued to work with fertility experts at the Miami Project. Preliminary attempts at artificial insemination were unsuccessful and frustrating. Lisa visited specialists at least once a week for blood tests and ultrasounds in hope of getting the timing just right.

"They tried everything they could to make us more comfortable with the procedures," Darrell recalls. "At one point we were in a 12 by 10 room with the lights turned low, blue and pink candles burning, and romantic music playing on a boom box. Nothing was working."

At the track in '97, the now Mopar-backed Darrell Gwynn team, piloted by Mike Dunn and tuned by Ken Veney, had an

LEFT: Darrell gets a ride in Rich Bickle's NASCAR Craftsman Truck Series racer. (Darrell Gwynn collection) ABOVE: One proud dad, Darrell holds his daughter, Katie. Darrell and Lisa endured years of tests and procedures before finally becoming pregnant with help from the Miami Project to Cure Paralysis. Katie was the twenty-fifth child born through the Miami Project and the first from a frozen embryo. "Of all the things I've been through in my life, this was by far the most dramatic," Darrell says. (Darrell Gwynn collection)

uneventful season. Despite Mike setting career-bests in speed (316.23 mph) and elapsed time (4.643 seconds), the team went winless for the first time since 1994 and finished eighth in the Winston point standings. The team's best finish was a runner-up to Joe Amato at the Gatornationals.

As the race season rolled to a close, Darrell and Lisa began looking into other pregnancy options, finally turning to in vitro fertilization. The process of harvesting Lisa's eggs, fertilizing them, and returning them to her uterus was a complicated one. She would need numerous injections over a period of weeks in an effort to overstimulate her system. The process of extracting sperm from Darrell was anything but pleasurable and could even be life threatening. The procedure dramatically raised his blood pressure, leaving him vulnerable to the risks of stroke and seizure.

"Let's just say it wasn't as much fun as the traditional way," Darrell says.

The first attempt at fertilization was scheduled for a Monday in early September. The Friday before, Darrell developed a painful kidney infection and was hospitalized with a 103-degree (Fahrenheit) fever that threatened the entire attempt. As Darrell battled the infection, doctors gave the couple one extra day—until Tuesday—before the window of opportunity would close and the process would have to start from the beginning.

For Lisa, starting over wasn't a realistic option. She was in her third year of medical school and didn't want to be pregnant during her residency. If this attempt didn't work, it would probably be several years before they would try again.

On Monday, Darrell's fever had dropped to 101 degrees and he was feeling a little better, but still not up to handling the necessary strain on his body. Three medical teams were working with the Gwynns. Lisa's fertility team was waiting in South Miami, while Darrell's fertility doctors worked with the team treating the kidney infection at Jackson Memorial.

"After crying and arguing and thinking I couldn't do it, Lisa was walking out of the room and I just said, 'Damn it. Let's do it,'" Darrell recalls. "At that moment, it looked like a pit stop at the Daytona 500—everyone went into action."

Darrell's procedure went without incident, and the sperm was taken to South Miami and injected into seventeen of Lisa's harvested eggs. By Tuesday morning, word came that fifteen had fertilized and now were considered pre-embryos.

The embryos were allowed to divide for three days before five were placed back into Lisa's uterus. The ten remaining embryos were frozen at -80 degrees Fahrenheit.

ABOVE: Jerry and several of his friends handled much of the construction of Darrell and Lisa's house in South Florida. Darrell and Lisa were often on site making decisions on everything from where light switches would go to all the other details involved in a customized home. (Darrell Gwynn collection)

Despite a positive pregnancy test and initial excitement, none of the embryos developed. Frustrated, but not without hope, Darrell and Lisa planned to try one more time before the end of the year.

In early October, the ten remaining frozen embryos were thawed. Only five survived the temperature change and were viable for implant.

"We decided to put all five in and see what happened," Lisa says. "If nothing happened, it wasn't meant to be at that time. Fortunately, one of the five embryos took and we were pregnant—finally."

"Of all the things that have happened in my life, those few days were by far the most dramatic," Darrell says. "The way everyone was standing by and things kept coming down to the last minute—it was all right out of a movie."

Unfortunately, the drama didn't end there. Early prenatal tests revealed the possibility of Down's syndrome in the developing child. "We wanted to be able to celebrate and enjoy the nine months, but we couldn't," Darrell says. "There could still be serious complications. We were happy, but it wasn't a total celebration. Not yet."

The definitive answer was available only through amniocentesis, a process in which doctors pierce the abdominal wall with a hollow needle and enter the uterus to extract fluid for testing. Fears that the procedure could lead to other complications, including the possibility of miscarriage, led Darrell and Lisa to decline the procedure. "There was nothing we could do but wait," Lisa says.

As the 1998 race season got underway, the team continued to improve, with Mike making it to the final round four times, including three in a row during a mid-season stretch. All four losses were to eventual Top Fuel champ Gary Scelzi, with one coming at the U.S. Nationals.

The team again improved on speed (320.97 mph) and time (4.586 seconds), but the extended winless streak continued. The combination of Darrell, Mike, and Ken had not visited victory lane since the 1996 Pennzoil Nationals.

In June, after nine months of worry, Darrell and Lisa finally got to fill another room in their new home. On June 26, Lisa gave birth

ABOVE: At a Miami Project roast, Darrell joins several other sports personalities in the festivities. Top from left: former Miami Dolphins coach Don Shula, NBA legend Julius "Dr. J" Erving, sports announcer Bob Costas, former Miami Dolphins running back Larry Csonka, and former Miami Dolphins linebacker Nick Buoniconti. Marc Buoniconti is next to Darrell in front. (Darrell Gwynn collection)

to a healthy baby girl. Katie Brianne Gwynn was welcomed with open arms, becoming the twenty-fifth child born through the Miami Project and the first in the program from a frozen embryo.

"We kept Katie's name a secret until she was born," Darrell says. "Everything we had done over the past several years had been so public. We just wanted something that was special to us. My mom, Lisa's mom, her aunt Diane, and Lisa's sister, Michelle, were all in the room when Katie was born, and everyone wanted to know her name. It was a wonderful moment. It was awesome."

Darrell called Jerry, who was with the team in St. Louis. A rain delay made for perfect timing: Darrell's car was next in line when the call came, and the announcement of Katie's birth was made over the public address system.

The effect on Darrell, who by undergoing the procedures had risked his life to have a child with Lisa, was immediate. "I saw him become a new person—more loving—right away," says Joan. "He was smiling all the time."

At the track, Darrell and the team viewed 1998 as the beginning of good things for the race team. "That was the year Lou Patane came on as the motor sports chief at Chrysler, and we felt really good about him being in that position," Darrell says. "Here was a guy who could control the budget and who knew drag racing. We felt like it was a great opportunity for our team to grow and become one of the elite programs in the Top Fuel division."

Full of promise, the new sponsorship was not without its difficulties, even from the beginning. "I think the people calling the shots with the Mopar program were more personality driven than results driven," Mike says. "The Mopar engineers wanted Ken and Darrell to do things according to Mopar research results, and we didn't always do that. We felt like we had tried some of those things already and we didn't need to waste time doing them again. They wanted to go a certain direction, and they wanted people who would go with them."

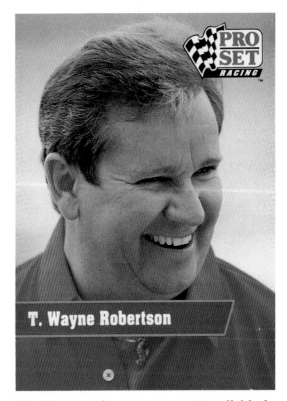

T. Wayne Robertson

Heading into the 1999 season, Darrell felt the team was close to championship form, and despite some tuning disagreements with Mopar, the sponsor appeared ready to renew its contract through the 2000 season. Darrell decided it was time to make the personal and financial commitment to go after the Winston title.

"We brought in Mike Sullivan, a very talented engineer who had owned the Dodge Pro Stock cars, and he was an immediate asset to the team," Darrell says. "He could look at the computer and instantly pick up things that guys with years of experience wouldn't notice. And of course, everyone on the crew was happier that we were spending more money."

The aggressive approach paid immediate dividends as the team

ABOVE: The team picture in victory lane at the Gatornationals includes
Jerry, Joan, Lisa, and little Katie. (Darrell Gwynn collection)

won the season opener in Pomona, getting ahead of the competition on the use of a popular new five-disc clutch being used by several of the top nitromethane teams. Mike Dunn held onto the points lead through the early part of the season, winning again in Gainesville, but the team struggled with consistency as the track conditions and weather changed.

"It was a year of being great on good tracks and not being able to hit our ass on bad ones," Darrell says. "And then the bottom dropped out."

Waiting to get official confirmation on the 2000 sponsor renewal, the team instead received an impersonal fax at five o'clock in the evening. Mopar was ending its relationship with Darrell Gwynn Racing at the end of the '99 season. The fourteen-year relationship had come to an abrupt end via an end-of-the-business-day fax. Everyone in the Gwynn camp was stunned.

"I was furious," Darrell says. "We were leading the points race. We had taken the necessary risks to go after a championship, and we had done everything Lou had asked us to do. I'd never heard of a team losing its sponsor while leading a points race."

Prior to Mopar's decision, Jerry Gwynn had approached Patane about the need to boost the team's $1.5 million budget in order to compete with the high-dollar Top Fuel teams owned by Kenny Bernstein and Don Prudhomme. Patane instructed Jerry to write a letter that could be taken to senior management, to explain the need to increase the race team's budget. Both Darrell and Jerry believed Patane was in their corner. But in an *Auto Week* magazine article, Darrell and Jerry explained what they later saw as a setup by Patane. "He'd kind of told us what to write," Jerry says.

"We wrote the letter and added some facts that kind of justified what he wanted us to write," Darrell adds. "It was all facts and you can't argue with facts. It was not a letter that I thought would get me in trouble. But that's probably what resulted in our 'execution.' The most shocking part was I didn't 'cc' anybody on the letter. I thought he'd read it and, if he had a problem with it, call me up and say 'This isn't what I asked for.' Or, 'Are you an idiot? Why did you send this?' Or, 'You know what? Change this and this and send it back to me.' Three days later, he called a 'town meeting' [at Chrysler]

ABOVE: Mike Dunn gives his trophy from the 1999 Winston Finals to first-time race-goer Cory Capece. Darrell and Cory had just met that day. "It was a wonderful night," Darrell says. Darrell and Cory still keep in touch. (Darrell Gwynn collection)

ABOVE: The "Darrell Gwynn posse" in the Daytona International Speedway garage area. Darrell's trips to NASCAR events at Daytona are a long-standing tradition. (Darrell Gwynn collection)

BELOW: Darrell with his grandmother Elaine Walker, Jerry and Joan, Mike and Sandy Dunn after Darrell was honored as a sports legend by the Miami Project. (Darrell Gwynn collection) **RIGHT:** While in Colorado for the 1999 Mile High Nationals in Denver, Darrell visited with victims of the Columbine High School shooting tragedy at Craig Hospital. Craig is recognized as one of the nation's premier facilities for the rehabilitation of patients with spinal cord and brain injuries. Here, Darrell talks with shooting victim Pat Ireland. (Darrell Gwynn collection)

and afterward they sent us this fax. Didn't even call us."

In addition to the Gwynns' request for more funds—they were looking to nearly double their budget—there were other factors in the Mopar decision. In the midst of massive employee layoffs, Mopar's parent company, DaimlerChrysler, was funding an expensive return to NASCAR Winston Cup Series racing. The Dodge Intrepid was planned for the 2001 racing season.

In his role as vice president of Dodge Motorsports Operations and Mopar Performance Parts, Patane hired Ray Evernham, former crew chief to four-time NASCAR champion Jeff Gordon, to spearhead the Dodge Winston Cup campaign. In an interesting turn of events, Patane retired from DaimlerChrysler in 2001, only to be hired as senior vice president of business operations by Evernham Motorsports, leaving the Gwynns to wonder if he had ever been in their corner at all.

Although Dodge remained in the NHRA with a Funny Car entry and a stable of Pro Stock cars, the big money was moving to NASCAR.

Despite its incredible disappointment, the team continued to

show championship form at the track, with Mike winning two more events—the Route 66 Nationals and the season finale in Pomona. The team also lowered the national elapsed time record to 4.503 seconds. "Pomona was bittersweet," Darrell recalls. "It felt great to win, but I had the feeling it might be our last win."

The team settled for a fourth-place finish in points, and no one stepped forward with a big enough budget to keep the team racing in 2000. NHRA leadership was in transition, and the sport's television package had been unattractive for several years, leaving top-dollar sponsorships at a premium.

"It was disappointing," Darrell says. "We knew where we were and what we had to do to get to the next level. Even if someone had come to the table with the same money we were getting from Mopar, we weren't going to do it. We had some offers to do it for less money and we probably could have put some things together, but none of us wanted to do it again unless the situation was right."

Darrell, Jerry, Mike, and Ken all agreed to sit it out together and see what happened. Although Mike continued to draw a salary

[149]

from Darrell Gwynn Racing, he certainly missed out on other, more lucrative opportunities.

"We were a good team," Mike said. "We had other offers, but Ken didn't want to change again and we were all confident that something would work out to keep us together. I'm sure it cost Darrell a lot of money to sit out the 2000 season and it cost me money to sit out, but we believed it was the right things to do."

Darrell, however, tried to make the best of his time off. "I got to do a lot of things I would not have had time to do if we were racing," Darrell says. "I went to a few late-model races. We took Katie to

Disney World. I enjoyed the time with my family."

By July 2000, it looked like the season was lost. No deals were on the table, and Mike's only time behind the wheel came as a fill-in for Joe Amato at the Winston Invitational. But then things started to change.

The NHRA's new system of penalties and a 90 percent nitromethane rule, requiring teams to cut back on the purity of the explosive fuel they were using, made significant reductions in the number of engine explosions and time-consuming cleanups. In July,

an attractive five-year television deal with ESPN was announced, and the new NHRA president, Tom Compton, quickly was earning a reputation as a leader who listened to the competitors.

Enter the world champion New York Yankees. Over the previous few seasons, the Gwynns had received several calls from a friend of Hank Steinbrenner, son of Yankees owner George Steinbrenner. The caller was representing Hank and inquiring about getting involved in drag racing. The first calls were about buying a car and possibly some parts. Hank was a student of the sport, having followed the NHRA for nearly thirty years. He had a particular fondness for Top Fuel dragsters.

"On July 17, we got a call from Hank and he felt it was time to go racing," Darrell says. "ESPN had just announced the new television package. He knew we were sitting on the sidelines, so he asked us to drive up to Tampa the following week and discuss the possibility of putting a team together. It was like the story of the dog chasing the truck—we caught the truck, now what do we do?"

Darrell called on some friends for help at the initial meeting with the Steinbrenners. Chuck Blossom, former president of Mac Tools, and Sean Thompson, a marketing professional whom Darrell had been working with, joined the Gwynns for the meeting. On the Steinbrenner side of the table were Hank, several attorneys, and representatives from the accounting firm of Price Waterhouse.

Hank took the floor first. "We were stunned with how much he knew about our history," Darrell says. "He knew what year I won Indy and what I ran. He was an avid reader. He even brought up a story from 1965, about my dad helping pull a guy out of a water-filled ditch during a race in Palm Beach. It felt like the FBI had been watching us our whole lives.

"It was kind of spooky, but flattering at the same time," Darrell continues. "When you've been out of racing for six months and you can't get potential sponsors to return your calls, you start wondering if anyone loves you or remembers what you did. You start

ABOVE: Darrell visits with four-time NASCAR Winston Cup Series champion Jeff Gordon in the NASCAR garage area. Gordon is a friend of Darrell's and is the honorary chairperson of the Darrell Gwynn Foundation. (Darrell Gwynn collection)

TOP LEFT: Darrell with, from left, Mike Dunn, Jerry, and Hank Steinbrenner in front of the trophy case on the day the contract with the New York Yankees was signed at the Gwynn race shop. (Darrell Gwynn collection)

TOP RIGHT: Darrell chats with Yankees legend Reggie Jackson soon after announcing the partnership with the Steinbrenners. (Don Gillespie, Darrell Gwynn collection)

BOTTOM RIGHT: Mike Dunn was Darrell's driver for nine seasons. (Don Gillespie, Darrell Gwynn collection) **BOTTOM LEFT:** New York Yankees team owner George Steinbrenner joins Darrell, Jerry, and Hank Steinbrenner at one of the team's first test sessions. (Don Gillespie, courtesy Darrell Gwynn)

wondering if you left any mark at all on the sport. So, when I left that first meeting, it made me feel like at least someone had been paying attention. It made me feel good about staying out of trouble and keeping my nose clean and someone recognizing it."

Darrell believes the Gwynn team staying together made the deal even more attractive to the Steinbrenners.

"The loyalty the team had shown while sitting out seemed to mean a lot to them," Darrell adds. "There were several exchanges of faxes and phone calls, and on August 3, they flew down on their private plane, we picked them up at the airport, and they came to the race shop to finalize a three-year $10 million deal, with an option for two additional years."

The Gwynns informed all of their associate sponsors, including Winnebago and Mac Tools, by way of a special overnight package. In addition to the announcement, each was sent a signed baseball and a Yankees cap along with other memorabilia. The announcement also helped close several pending deals, as talks with General Motors wrapped up, with GM Mobility joining the Gwynn stable of associate sponsors.

The official announcement came on the front page of the August 29 USA Today sports section. The car was unveiled a few days later at the U.S. Nationals in Indy.

With an inventory of fresh parts, including twelve new motors, the team set a three-race schedule for 2000—Dallas, Houston, and Pomona—hoping to get adjusted to the new 90 percent rule in plenty of time for a championship run in 2001. Two test dates in Gainesville, Florida, however, left the team unsure of its future.

"We attempted about thirty runs over two separate sessions, including one with George and Hank in attendance," Darrell says. "I don't think we ever got past 100 feet without smoking the tires. We had no idea what was going on. With a new combination, a new team, a bunch of new parts, not having raced for months—and never under the 90 percent rule—we weren't sure if it was not

hooking up or was hooking up too much. We didn't know if we needed a wheelie bar. We didn't know if we needed to raise the motor or lower the motor. We didn't know if we had the right tune-up. These are just the things that start going through a crew chief's mind when you're not running well.

"To Ken's credit, he was probably right on the money with his setup, but the track just wasn't in great shape on those weekends,"

Darrell adds. "We didn't think we had things screwed up, and without other cars to measure ourselves against, we made plans to pick another test spot. We knew we couldn't show up at our first race with the Yankees on the side of the car and not be able to get down the racetrack."

So, the team hauled the car to Memphis for a Monday test date following the NHRA national event at Memphis Motorsports Park. On the first run, Ken asked Mike to go to the 330-foot mark. The numbers were impressive. On the next run, the direction was to take it to half track. The numbers were "warp speed" faster than anyone had run that weekend. Everyone assumed the clocks must have malfunctioned because computer readouts were showing incredible times. The third time the car went down the track, it ran an eye-popping 4.54.

The first real test for the team, however, would come in late October as they debuted the new Yankees machine at the Matco Tools Supernationals in Houston. On the first qualifying run, the car broke a blower belt in the middle of good run. At the Friday night qualifying session, with Darrell not yet at the track, the car stunned the field with a run of 4.53 at 322 mph, by far the best numbers ever run under the new 90 percent rule.

"I remember being in the van and the phone rang," Darrell says. "My dad was going absolutely nuts on the other end. He was saying 'You aren't going to believe what the car just did.' To that point, I don't think anyone had run over 320 mph under the 90 percent rule. My dad was so pumped up. I could still hear track announcer Bob Frey in the background on the PA saying 'Unbelievable.' You could just feel the emotion and the excitement."

Darrell immediately called Hank. "His response was 'How did you guys do that?'" Darrell says. "He knew what it took to pull that off in a Top Fuel car, and he was as surprised as the rest of us."

Although Mike wasn't able to earn a victory in any of the team's test events in 2000, he did qualify number one at all three races and clearly emerged as one of the favorites to compete for the championship in 2001.

"I really felt like we had our dream team in place for 2001," Darrell says. "We had Mike, Ken, and Mike Sullivan, and we added another talented guy in Todd Smith. And to top it off, we were racing with the New York Yankees on the side of the car. We had a budget that allowed us to pay guys what they were worth, the crew felt comfortable moving their families to South Florida, and we felt good about where we were headed as a team."

At Gainesville, the pressure started to build. "George and Hank were coming to the race, and we had no idea how to handle it," Darrell says. "We didn't know whether to throw up a tent and serve hot dogs, buy a suite and serve steak, or let George stand in the rain. Whatever choice we made, we felt like it would be the wrong one."

The Steinbrenners bought one of the track suites for the weekend, inviting Darrell's family to join them. At a meeting following the race, however, George let Darrell know that he thought they were spending too much money.

"He thought we were all staying at the Ritz-Carlton, flying to races in Lear jets, and inviting all our friends out to the track to party," Darrell says. "I finally interrupted and told him he was wasting his time on this topic. I told him that my father was handling the money as if he were George Steinbrenner Jr., not allowing anyone to take advantage of the budget. He was quiet for a minute, but then he said 'I believe you.'"

But the tension was definitely increasing, and George Steinbrenner's disenchantment with the race team continued to grow. There were rumblings that he wanted to change the contract from a three-year deal to a one-year deal. To push the issue, Darrell says he stopped all payments to the team, forcing them to choose between shutting down and going to court or continuing to chase the championship with no idea where the money would come from. Not wanting to bring negative attention to the team, Darrell made the decision to keep the Yankees' colors on the car.

Concerned with the weakened financial status of the team and Steinbrenner hobbling the team's cash flow, Darrell also feared a midsummer performance letdown, a familiar problem that had cursed his race team over the years. Notoriously fast early in the season under ideal conditions, Gwynn Racing had a history of wilting in the summer heat and then coming on strong again late in the season.

"We won in Atlanta with Hank at the race, but I sensed the same things coming on," Darrell says. "In the middle of the day on hot summer afternoons, the competition saw us as easy targets. It's always been a problem for drag racers to get down a hot racetrack—it is one of the hardest things to do in the world. And it seemed to be magnified in 2001 by the pressure to succeed and by the success we were having on good tracks."

As the team began to struggle, George Steinbrenner stuck with a strategy he had employed so often with his baseball teams—he wanted to fire the manager. As the U.S. Nationals approached, the Gwynns were summoned to meet with the Steinbrenners in Tampa. Although many topics were on the table, the conversation finally turned ugly when George directed Darrell to fire crew chief Ken Veney.

Darrell refused, saying, "We are heading to the biggest race of the year, and I want the best chance to win that race. Ken Veney gives me the best chance. Unless you have a better answer, Ken is the crew chief."

Steinbrenner threw his hands in the air and responded, "See, I knew you hired your friends. Now, you are afraid to make changes. You'll never get anywhere with this team if you are afraid to make changes."

When the meeting was over, Ken Veney was still the crew chief, but the Gwynn-Steinbrenner partnership was crumbling.

The team would make it all the way to the finals at Indy, vindicating Darrell's decision to stick with Veney. The U.S. Nationals, however, would be remembered for much more than a trip to the finals

or the showdown with "the Boss." For before he ever arrived at Indy in 2001, Darrell's friends had been planning a special day for him. For Darrell, it would be a chance to be the Kid again.

Years earlier, former Gwynn Racing employee Mike Gerry and Dennis Sarmento, a friend and owner of Sarmento Fabrication, had tossed around the idea of building a special dragster for Darrell that he could drive despite his limitations. Sketches were drawn as early as 1992.

Early in 2001, Gerry reintroduced the idea to his boss, Jeff Whittle. Whittle owned Recreation Development Company and wanted to get more involved in drag racing. The two discussed the possibilities and the stumbling blocks, especially in the areas of steering. After some initial hesitation, Whittle was on board. He asked Gerry to put together preliminary specs and a cost breakdown.

In June, Gerry turned to some of the experts in drag racing in order to make the Labor Day deadline. The car would not only be a trib-

"He's been such an inspiration to so many people, we decided to give him the greatest birthday present possible—a chance to make another ¼-mile pass down IRP during the U.S. Nationals," says Mike Gerry.

ute to Darrell, but a surprise fortieth birthday present as well. Gerry called Sarmento and reminded him of their 10-year-old conversation. Sarmento was in. Gerry then contacted Kevin Vornhagen, one of the best painters in the business. Vornhagen was in. The calls continued and the team kept growing. Whether it was with money, products, or services, everyone seemed to want to help. The project soon involved Harry Burkholder, Eric Reyes, Elliott Taylor, Richard Steinke, Jim Moore, and many more.

Darrell knew nothing about the car and was always in or around his wheelchair, so Jerry was forced to sneak measurements using his arm as a makeshift ruler. The measurements would later help in the design of the steering system and the seating area.

The 222-inch Super Comp—style dragster took a month and ten days to complete and was tested in the parking lot of RDC on August 25. The car, carrying the paint scheme combining Darrell's former and current sponsors, was created with such detail that it could pass NHRA tech inspection if not for the detached roll bar feature that allowed Darrell access to the vehicle.

Constructed with chrome moly tubing, the car was equipped with a hand-controlled throttle, steering, and braking unit. Resting on 33-inch Goodyear tires, the six 8-volt batteries would push the car to more than 20 mph. The front tires were custom-made by Amerityre, with Darrell's name molded on the side. The car was delivered to Indianapolis Raceway Park in an enclosed trailer.

"I've been associated with the Gwynns since Darrell began driving in the Sportsman ranks," Gerry says. "I helped build some of his first chassis, including the Miami Vice dragster he ran in the eighties. He's been such an inspiration to so many people, we decided to give him the greatest birthday present possible—a chance to make another 1/4-mile pass down IRP during the U.S. Nationals."

Despite the effort to keep the car a surprise, Darrell began sensing something was up as he noticed several secretive conversations going on around the racetrack and groups of people leaving the pit

area. It was the NHRA's fiftieth anniversary season, and Darrell's fortieth birthday offered fair game for some kind of spectacular prank. He just wasn't quite sure what it was.

Later in the afternoon, Darrell was told he was needed at the circle track adjoining the drag strip at IRP. Darrell's business manager, Bob Abdellah, insisted Darrell take a wheelchair shuttle—something he never did on his own. On the way, Bob was told via radio that not everyone was in place and he had to buy some time, so he pretended to have forgotten something back at the pit area.

"On the way, I could hear the chatter going back and forth on the radio, so I knew something was happening," Darrell says. "As we finally got over to the circle track, there was a crowd of people and I started recognizing a lot of familiar faces from my past. Then I saw Lisa and Katie and I knew something special was happening—they hadn't even been planning to come to Indy. When everyone moved away and I saw the car, I just couldn't believe it."

The crowd broke into a chorus of "Happy Birthday."

LEFT: Knowing how much worse things could have been, Joan Gwynn is accepting and focused on the future after the horrific accident that befell her son: "I was never mad about what happened to Darrell. I was sad, but I knew as long as he was alive, we could still make memories." (Don Gillespie, Darrell Gwynn collection) **ABOVE:** Former Gwynn racing crew member Mike Gerry works on a surprise gift for Darrell's fortieth birthday—an electric dragster. (Darrell Gwynn collection)

LEFT: Darrell with the crew that delivered the electric dragster to Indy. From left: Julie Gerry, Mike Gerry, Jeff Whittle, Shelly Whittle, Michelle Wagner, Wade Wagner, Bobbi Whittle, Greg Whittle, and Eric Reyes. (Don Gillespie, Darrell Gwynn collection) **BELOW:** Darrell test drives the electric dragster on the circle track at Indianapolis Raceway Park. Says friend and business manager Bob Abdellah, "When he finally stopped, he appeared to be five years younger." (Don Gillespie, Darrell Gwynn collection)

Mike Gerry walked over to Darrell and gave him the news: "Happy birthday, little buddy. This car is yours. You're driving it tonight." Darrell began to cry.

As the crowd continued to sing, Darrell was lowered into his new hot rod. Three-year-old Katie's eyes were as big as saucers as her daddy put on his helmet. Some adjustments were needed to the joy-stick steering, a glitch Jerry fixed in no time. Within minutes, Darrell was taking his new car for a counterclockwise test drive around the circle track.

"When he finally stopped, he seemed to be five years younger," Abdellah says.

But the trip down the 1/4 mile almost didn't happen. A downpour had flooded much of the pit area Friday morning, creating havoc with the schedule. With Darrell slated to run the car Friday night, NHRA vice president of racing operations Graham Light was threatening to cancel the pass due to time constraints.

Jerry stepped in and convinced Light that the event had to go on—so many people had poured their hearts and souls into the project and traveled from all over the country to see the final result. Light

finally agreed.

"The NHRA was great," Darrell says. "This was their fiftieth anniversary, and Garlits and Muldowney were there to race. They had a lot going on, and they still were flexible enough to let me make one pass down the 1/4 mile."

Darrell was wheeled up to the Christmas tree and greeted by several other drivers, including Don Prudhomme and John Force. Just then, little Katie walked over, extended her tiny finger in the air and said "You're number one, Daddy." Sharing a playfulness found throughout the Gwynn family and piercing blue eyes that come straight from her dad, Katie was thrilled to see Darrell seated behind the wheel.

"For Katie to get to see me in a race car meant so much," Darrell says.

Full of pride, Jerry walked over and gave Darrell the signature handshake he had given so many times during Darrell's career.

"So much love went into making that night special," Jerry says. "It was unforgettable."

As Darrell staged the car, the crowd came to their feet—cheering, crying, and chanting—as a video commemorating Darrell's career played on the big screen to the music of Michael Bolton's "Back on My Feet Again."

Lisa turned away.

"It was a real emotional night for me," Lisa says. "I was very happy for Darrell, but it also brought back a lot of emotions. Without really knowing it, our family has buried a lot of difficult memories and with the crowd cheering and the video playing and the music behind it all, I was just flooded with emotions. I wanted to see Darrell go down the track, but I didn't want to see the video or listen to the song. All of the memories—good and bad—came back at once."

Comforted by longtime friend Linda Vaughn, Lisa turned and watched Darrell finish the run.

Darrell loved the feeling of being back in the car. "When I went through the water, I wanted to give it a little pop and hear the noise a Top Fuel dragster makes. It didn't matter that I wasn't going near fast enough—just to feel that way again was incredible," Darrell says. "The car was so quiet, I could hear all the cheers from the crowd. I was going so slow, but I wished I could have gone even slower, just to keep the moment going a little longer."

The crowd stayed on their feet as Darrell came down the return road with his family following close behind in a golf cart.

A little more than a decade earlier, Darrell thought he might never make another trip down the 1/4 mile in a race car. On August 31, 2001, his friends and family made sure he did.

ABOVE: Darrell brings the car back down the return road to a standing ovation at Indy. Says Darrell of the experience: "For the first time in my life, I wish I had gone slower." (Don Gillespie, Darrell Gwynn collection)

Epilogue

In 2001, Darrell Gwynn Racing continued to compete in the elite NHRA Top Fuel division. Still wearing New York Yankees pinstripes, despite being, as Darrell puts it, "fired more times than Billy Martin," the team finished fourth in Winston points. As part of the NHRA's 50th Anniversary celebration, Darrell was listed as number thirty-two on the sanctioning body's list of fifty all-time greats.

Lisa, who had graduated from medical school in 1998, completed her pediatrics residency in 2001 and began practicing in the South Florida cities of Hollywood and Pembroke Pines, as her parents, Wayne and Adrianne, moved into the family home to help care for Katie.

Mike Dunn left the team in 2002 after nine years with the Gwynns and went to work as part of the ESPN television team covering the NHRA. With an ever-tightening budget, the team could no longer afford to keep Ken Veney and Mike Sullivan. Full-time crew chief duties were turned over to Todd Smith.

Andrew Cowin, son of Australian drag racer Graeme Cowin, brought some funding to the team and strapped into the Yankee dragster for the 2002 season. Getting off to a quick start, Andrew qualified the car number one at the season opener with a track ET record at Pomona, a mark that would stand for the entire season. Andrew went on to qualify number one three more times, setting career bests in speed and ET, but he never found victory lane. He finished eighth in points, but would not return in 2003 as the team continued to search for additional funding.

Darrell and his family also started working toward a new dream in 2002, forming the Darrell Gwynn Foundation in an effort to prevent, provide for, and ultimately cure spinal cord injuries and aid research funding for spinal cord injuries and other debilitating illnesses. Darrell had already been active in this arena, and the foundation allowed him to formalize his many charitable activities. With the entire Gwynn family on the foundation's board of directors, the foundation also boasts of participation from NASCAR Winston Cup champion team owner Joe Gibbs and four-time NASCAR Winston Cup Series champion Jeff Gordon.

As 2003 rolled around, Darrell and Lisa took time out to renew their wedding vows at a small private ceremony in front of their parents and Katie.

"Darrell told me that we were going to dinner with his parents and we had to go pick them up," Lisa explains. "When we got there, the house was filled with candles, Katie had flowers, and our pastor, Max Helton, was on the speakerphone to help us with the ceremony. It was beautiful."

On the track, Darrell came within days of parking the hot rod forever. But shortly before the season opener in Pomona, Darrell teamed with veteran Cory McClenathan and Cory's sponsor Berryman Products for yet another run at the elusive Top Fuel championship in 2003.

In explaining his redefined relationship with the Yankees, Darrell says, "They are still with us, but have given us room to grow in other directions."

[159]

LEFT: Katie gets to see Darrell in a way she has only seen in pictures. "For Katie to see me in a race car meant so much," Darrell says. (Don Gillespie, Darrell Gwynn collection) **ABOVE:** At track with the family in 1999. (Darrell Gwynn collection)

focused my energy on getting things done. That has never changed."

There still are occasional bad days and frustrating moments, but Darrell rolls past them by staying on the move—his wheelchair is in constant motion—and keeping a twisted sense of humor about life (a decal on his wheelchair reads "Crashing Sucks").

"There are still days when I am not comfortable being me," Darrell says. "Especially when I am trying to explain something to someone that I used to be able to do myself. But I have an amazing, beautiful wife, a daughter that makes me smile all day, and a network of family and friends that show me more love than I could ever repay. Most of my days are good days. Some are great days. That's what keeps me going."

So, can Darrell and Lisa picture life beyond racing?

"We talk about life without racing all the time," Lisa says. "But somehow we keep getting drawn back into it year after year. Darrell has some new projects now that hopefully will lead to more opportunities after racing."

To that end, the family has purchased land in the Florida Keys, a photo of which sits at eye level on Darrell's desk. In preparation for his time away from the 1/4 mile, Darrell already has tried out his latest gadget—a Penn reel with Electromate assistance for his wheelchair-mounted fishing rod. A couple of unfortunate Florida grouper already have marked the beginning of some serious fishing.

Darrell continues to endure therapy once a week, with an emphasis on maintenance rather than improvement.

"My schedule makes doing any more than that a little difficult, but the truth is I have never liked being in the hospital atmosphere," Darrell says. "I don't want to be there. It brings back too many difficult memories. That's why my weekly therapy routine is conducted in the race shop. I'm more comfortable there."

And not unlike his early days on the road, Darrell spends his late-night hours lying in bed, making lists of things he wants to accomplish in the coming days.

"I make lists like I'm not hurt," Darrell explains. "I've always

ABOVE: Plans to build a new home on this land purchased by Darrell and Lisa in the Florida Keys keeps Darrell motivated. This photo sits on his desk. (Darrell Gwynn collection) RIGHT: How much does Katie mean to Darrell? Wearing a mustache for years, Darrell shaved it when it meant Katie would kiss Daddy more often. (Darrell Gwynn collection)